New Daylight

Edited by Naomi Starkey   January–April 2006

Suggestions for using *New Daylight*

Find a regular time and place, if possible, where you can read and pray undisturbed. Before you begin, take time to be still and perhaps use the BRF prayer. Then read the Bible passage slowly (try reading it aloud if you find it over-familiar), followed by the comment. You can also use *New Daylight* for group study and discussion, if you prefer.

The prayer or point for reflection can be a starting point for your own meditation and prayer. Many people like to keep a journal to record their thoughts about a Bible passage and items for prayer. In *New Daylight* we also note the Sundays and special festivals from the Church calendar, to keep in step with the Christian year.

New Daylight and the Bible

New Daylight contributors use a range of Bible versions, and you will find a list of the versions used in each issue at the back of the notes on page 154. You are welcome to use your own preferred version alongside the passage printed in the notes, and this can be particularly helpful if the Bible text has been abridged.

New Daylight affirms that the whole of the Bible is God's revelation to us, and we should read, reflect on and learn from every part of both Old and New Testaments. Usually the printed comment presents a straightforward 'thought for the day', but sometimes it may also raise questions rather than simply providing answers, as we wrestle with some of the more difficult passages of Scripture.

Writers in this issue

Gordon Giles is a vicar in Enfield, north-west London, previously based at St Paul's Cathedral where his work involved musical and liturgical responsibilities. Trained in music, philosophy and theology, he was ordained in the Anglican Church in 1995. He has written *The Music of Praise* and *The Harmony of Heaven* for BRF.

Jenny Robertson is a writer whose books for children and adults have been widely translated. She has written *Strength of the Hills* and *Windows to Eternity* for BRF. After a number of years spent working in Russia and Poland, she and her husband are now based in Barcelona, Spain.

David Winter is retired from parish ministry. An honorary Canon of Christ Church, Oxford, he is well known as a writer and broadcaster. His most recent book for BRF is *Old Words, New Life*. He is a Series Editor of *The People's Bible Commentary*.

Tony Horsfall is a freelance trainer and associate of EQUIP, a missions programme based at Bawtry Hall near Doncaster. He is an elder of his local church in West Yorkshire, and regularly travels abroad leading retreats and Quiet Days. He has written *Song of the Shepherd* for BRF.

Stephen Rand, after working for Tearfund for 25 years, is now giving his time to work for Jubilee Debt Campaign, while he and his wife Susan help to lead a church in Wimbledon that meets to worship in the busiest cinema in the country!

Helen Julian CSF is an Anglican Franciscan sister, a member of the Community of St Francis, and presently serving as Minister Provincial for her community. She has written *Living the Gospel* and *The Lindisfarne Icon* for BRF.

Peter Graves is Minister of Wesley Methodist Church, Cambridge, and Chaplain to Methodist students at the University. He was formerly Superintendent of the Methodist Central Hall, Westminster.

Veronica Zundel is an Oxford graduate, writer and journalist. She lives with her husband and young son in North London, where they belong to the Mennonite Church.

Adrian Plass is an internationally popular writer and speaker. His most recent book for BRF is *When You Walk*.

Further BRF reading for this issue

For more in-depth coverage of some of the passages in these
Bible reading notes, we recommend the following titles:

PSALMS 1–72

THE PEOPLE'S
BIBLE COMMENTARY

**DONALD
COGGAN**

A BIBLE COMMENTARY FOR EVERY DAY

1 84101 031 6, £8.99

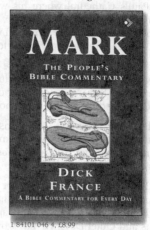

MARK

THE PEOPLE'S
BIBLE COMMENTARY

**DICK
FRANCE**

A BIBLE COMMENTARY FOR EVERY DAY

1 84101 046 4, £8.99

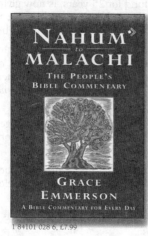

NAHUM to MALACHI

THE PEOPLE'S
BIBLE COMMENTARY

**GRACE
EMMERSON**

A BIBLE COMMENTARY FOR EVERY DAY

1 84101 028 6, £7.99

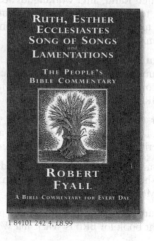

RUTH, ESTHER ECCLESIASTES SONG OF SONGS and LAMENTATIONS

THE PEOPLE'S
BIBLE COMMENTARY

**ROBERT
FYALL**

A BIBLE COMMENTARY FOR EVERY DAY

1 84101 242 4, £8.99

Naomi Starkey writes...

Responding to letters from *New Daylight* readers is one of the more interesting and, at times, challenging parts of my job! I have been moved to hear how the notes have helped people through difficult experiences, encouraged by a simple note of thanks, or challenged by a hard-hitting query.

Some questions do crop up more regularly than others, so I thought I would take the opportunity here to tackle four of them:

Q. In which countries are the notes distributed?

A. There are too many countries for a complete list, but I can state that copies are mailed to every continent except Antarctica.

Q. Why does *New Daylight* no longer follow the Sunday lectionary readings?

A. We decided to end this practice so as to enable contributors to work on a Bible passage or theme without interruption for a week or more. We still note the 'lectionary Gospel' for each year, aiming to explore Matthew, Mark or Luke during the relevant twelve months.

Q. Why do you only highlight some of the festivals in the Church calendar?

A. We highlight Sundays and 'red letter' festivals in the Church of England calendar as footnotes in every issue. We always provide special readings for Lent (at least Ash Wednesday), Holy Week and Easter, Christmas, Remembrance Sunday, and Women's World Day of Prayer. I choose to highlight a certain number of other festivals each year, with relevant readings . In the previous issue, for example, 'The gift of the Bible' coincided with the commemorations of Jerome (30 September) and William Tyndale (6 October).

Q. Why aren't the comments linked to events in the news?

A. The notes are commissioned around two years ahead of publication and edited about a year beforehand, due to a range of factors—ensuring that contributors have time for writing, the demands of our own publishing schedules and (not least) the logistics of shipping overseas (see the first question!).

Thank you to each reader who has raised these and many other issues. May *New Daylight* continue to provide you with food for thought!

The BRF Prayer

Almighty God,
you have taught us that your word is a lamp for our feet
and a light for our path. Help us, and all who prayerfully
read your word, to deepen our fellowship with each other
through your love. And in so doing may we come to know you
more fully, love you more truly, and follow more faithfully in
the steps of your son Jesus Christ, who lives and reigns with
you and the Holy Spirit, one God for evermore. Amen.

Psalms 1—19

The Psalms are the ancestors of the hymns we sing in church. Mostly attributed to King David—giant-killer, shepherd and harpist of the Old Testament—they cover a range of experiences and emotions that is unrivalled in world literature. They can be read quietly alone or formally incorporated into a daily pattern of praise and prayer, as the Anglican and Roman Catholic Churches have done for centuries. Archbishop Cranmer made the new 'Church of England' say or sing the whole psalter each month. In our reflections over the next fortnight, therefore, we are, to some extent, keeping pace with the BCP lectionary!

The chosen psalms with which we now journey into 2006 are a rich store of humanity and theology. Our creator God, the central figure in the universe, is the one to whom the psalmist calls in sorrow and in joy. Sometimes God seems distant, inaccessible, wilfully ignorant of the behaviour of those who torment his people. At other times we realize that God does stand up for the poor, oppressed and vulnerable. God is our shelter, our stronghold, our rock. We are invited to delight in God's laughter, the happiness of his people and the downfall of his enemies. In these psalms we find an emphasis on the nature of goodness: how to be good and what should or does happen to those who obey God and those who do not. Such a wealth of spiritual resources makes the psalms so human, so inspiring and so great.

They are also the word of God, profound insights into existence and eternity, lying at the heart of our Bibles. They speak of something David could barely imagine, but which we have seen and heard: the coming of Christ. When Charles Jennens compiled the text of Handel's *Messiah*, he drew extensively on the early psalms, emphasizing the prophecies they contain. As we read them, we see Jesus emerging through these words of worship and marvel at the insights into his ministry and mission embedded within them.

We never tire of the Psalms. They don't change, but our circumstances do. Like Jesus himself, they remain relevant and real, speaking afresh to every generation—sometimes piercing the complacency of modern morals, at other times giving assurance and hope. It is hard to think of a better way to begin a new year. May we be challenged and inspired by them again and again.

Gordon Giles

7

New Year happiness

Happy are those who do not follow the advice of the wicked, or take the path that sinners tread, or sit in the seat of scoffers; but their delight is in the law of the Lord, and on his law they meditate day and night. They are like trees planted by streams of water, which yield their fruit in its season, and their leaves do not wither. In all that they do, they prosper.

Happy New Year! In greeting 2006, we can welcome the first lines of this, the first psalm, with joy. It opens with the word 'happy', and so we should be as we look forward to what lies ahead. Perhaps you have made resolutions, or perhaps you have resolved not to, but I am sure you will agree that this year should not involve following the advice of the wicked, nor treading the path of sinners, nor sitting with the cynical. Now that will be easy, won't it?!

The psalmist makes it seem so straightforward and obvious: 'avoid wickedness and you will be fine'. Yes indeed, that must be true. Except, of course, there are some very holy people about, who have endured terrible hardship, and others who appear to prosper in spite of their evil deeds. Others suffer for no apparent reason. A year ago, for example, we were agonizing over the terrible earthquake and tsunami in South East Asia, which meant that tens of thousands died. Nor is it always

easy, in the midst of secular values, religious fanaticism and international suspicion to remain positive, peaceable and patient. Yet, in the face of such difficulties, these lines from Psalm 1 must ring out as guidelines for the year ahead. It is so easy to scoff cynically at the world and our leaders and lose sight of the law of God, which should instruct our daily, national and international relationships, leading us all in the paths of peace and goodwill. We are still in the midst of the Christmas season, when we celebrate the coming of Christ—the epitome of goodness, truth and peace—into our troubled world.

Sunday reflection

Let us always sing of a righteous God, a vision of whose justice is set forth in Psalms. This is the hope we set before us as we journey joyfully into the New Year.

GG

Why do the nations rage?

Why do the nations conspire, and the peoples plot in vain? The kings of the earth set themselves, and the rulers take counsel together, against the Lord and his anointed, saying, 'Let us burst their bonds asunder, and cast their cords from us.' He who sits in the heavens laughs; the Lord has them in derision.

We laugh in various ways: we can laugh at a joke or a clown or someone's wit. More sophisticated is irony or satire, which somehow reveals a truth or exposes hypocrisy or deceit. Much humour seems to be of this kind today as sitcoms and comedians like to use the absurdities of life or politics to get laughs, and possibly even to change public opinion. Wit and laughter are powerful weapons, and many regimes have tried to control humorists. A well-observed cartoon can puncture the inflated pride of social or political self-importance.

Then there is the kind of laughter that does not signify amusement. Mockery is cruel, it is laughing at rather than laughing with, and is dismissive of its victims. It is, as the psalmist puts it, 'derisive'. Apparently, God indulges in this belittling of those who dismiss him. This scene is portrayed musically by Handel in his *Messiah* as 'Why do the nations rage together?', 'Let us break their bonds' and 'He that dwelleth in heaven'. We also find it in Bernstein's *Chichester Psalms*, the text of which is interspersed with chunks of Psalm 23 ('The Lord is my shepherd'). However, here, we are not bemoaning the fact that nations wage war (which is lamentable, of course), but instead are seeing how God reacts to an apparent conspiracy to remove him from the game. Unlike children in a playground, God and his representatives are not to be ignored, sent to Coventry, to be heard and seen no more. The Godly power of which the conspirators are jealous is not denied. There is to be a revolution, a seizure of power instead. They are trying to break the cords by which they feel bound in a bid for freedom.

What does God do? He laughs. He laughs at their stupidity, mocks their arrogance and dismisses their pride.

Prayer

God, in you alone is true freedom, wisdom and value. Make us laugh for joy in the face of your love. Amen

GG

Thou shalt dash them

I will tell of the decree of the Lord: He said to me, 'You are my son; today I have begotten you. Ask of me, and I will make the nations your heritage, and the ends of the earth your possession. You shall break them with a rod of iron, and dash them in pieces like a potter's vessel.' … Happy are all who take refuge in him.

We continue with Psalm 2, in which God derides those who dismiss him and in which the figure of his anointed one seems to show a new way forward. For Christians, this is a foretaste of Christ, seen in Psalms. The writer of Hebrews is clear when he quotes this very passage in Hebrews 1:5, stating clearly that Jesus is the anointed one of God, higher than even the angels. Handel quotes this text in his *Messiah* and those who know the work may be able to hear in their heads that wonderful aria 'Thou shalt break them, and dash them, in pieces with a rod of iron, like a potter's vessel'. The music is authoritative, strident almost, conveying the power that God is here bestowing on his anointed Messiah.

In these words, we have the counter-revolution: God's response in the battlefield of sin. Following from yesterday's segment, we see that God does not merely laugh at the revolutionary tendencies of his deriders: he takes them on. He sends in the troops or, rather, the supreme trooper in the war against sin: his only begotten Son, Jesus Christ. Jesus, the Messiah (which means 'anointed one'), is to be king of the nations, ruler to the ends of the Earth, and Matthew echoes these words when he records Jesus sending the disciples out as his evangelists: 'All authority in heaven and on earth has been given to me. Go therefore and make disciples of all nations… teaching them to obey everything that I have commanded you' (Matthew 28:18–20). Psalm 2 foresees it, Matthew records it happening and Hebrews looks back and makes the connection. Thus, we can observe God's purposes worked out and carried out over a great span of history.

Prayer

O Lord our Messiah, make us happy to take refuge in you, for you are our King, now and forever. Amen

GG

Lead me, Lord

But I, through the abundance of your steadfast love, will enter your house, I will bow down towards your holy temple in awe of you. Lead me, O Lord, in your righteousness because of my enemies; make your way straight before me.... But let all who take refuge in you rejoice; let them ever sing for joy. Spread your protection over them, so that those who love your name may exult in you.

Samuel Sebastian Wesley (1810–76) set some of these lines from Psalm 5 to music. 'Lead me Lord' is actually part of a much longer piece called 'Praise the Lord my soul', which mostly uses words from Psalm 103. Wesley was the illegitimate son of Samuel Wesley, the son of the great Charles Wesley, brother of John Wesley, whose conversion inspired the founding of the Methodist Church. S.S. Wesley's famous piece, with its fluid melody, illustrates the simple prayer that we be led by our Lord in the straight way.

As well as the beautiful music, we might be reminded of Jesus' warning that 'the gate is narrow and the road is hard that leads to life, and there are few who find it' (Matthew 7:14). Yet it is the steadfast love of the Lord that we can rely on to lead us clearly in the paths of righteousness and right behaviour. Many today say that life is so complicated that it is hard to know how to act or how to live our lives. It is true that there are many distractions, many alternative lifestyles, many opposing ethical views and plenty of dilemmas with which to wrestle. It is also surely part of our Christian calling that we should engage with the complexities of our age—the difficult questions about the right to live or die and how to make love and not war. It is our duty to engage with these issues and our calling to strive to discover the narrow path through them. Sometimes the path is so narrow we can barely make it out, so that the narrow way begins to feel more like a tightrope. We never walk alone, though, as God in Christ leads us, through thick and thin, if only we would take refuge in him, place our hand in his and follow him.

Prayer

Lead me, Lord, through thick and thin. Amen

GG

11

Kings and babes

O Lord, our Sovereign, how majestic is your name in all the earth! You have set your glory above the heavens. Out of the mouths of babes and infants you have founded a bulwark because of your foes, to silence the enemy and the avenger. When I look at your heavens, the work of your fingers, the moon and the stars that you have established; what are human beings that you are mindful of them, mortals that you care for them?

In Miles Coverdale's translation of Psalm 8, which we find in the *Book of Common Prayer*, this psalm opens in a delightful way that has brought a smile to the lips of many generations of choristers: 'O Lord our Governor, how excellent is thy name in all the world.' It does have a certain ring to it that can remind us of stereotypical London taxi drivers accepting a fare from the 'guv'nor'! Certainly this is a psalm that can make us smile for other reasons as it speaks of God as the kind of king who delights in creation and whom we may presume to call 'our Sovereign'. Yes, 'this is our God, the servant King', as Graham Kendrick famously put it.

Psalm 8 is used liturgically on Christmas Day and Ascension Day—happy feast days on which we extol the kingship of Christ and his power and glory revealed for the good of all creation. The ascended Christ reigns on high, but the babe of Bethlehem—'the newborn king' of whom we sang so recently at our carol services— is still very much in our thoughts. Tomorrow we celebrate Epiphany, when the magi came to pay homage to the child 'born a king on Bethlehem plain'. In popular imagination, the magi are often characterized as 'we three kings' from the East. Yet, in their kingship, in Christ's kingship and in the kingship presented in this psalm, there is humility and accessibility, even to young children, who praise God from the cradle. Indeed, to look at any baby is to look at creation. The moon and the stars are heavenly wonders, for sure, but so too are the tiny fingers of a newborn baby.

Prayer

God our King, we thank you that you care for us and in Christ serve us in the very creation in which you delight!

GG

Kings of the earth

Yet you have made them [humans] a little lower than God, and crowned them with glory and honour. You have given them dominion over the works of your hands; you have put all things under their feet, all sheep and oxen, and also the beasts of the field, the birds of the air, and the fish of the sea, whatever passes along the paths of the seas. O Lord, our Sovereign, how majestic is your name in all the earth!

Epiphany is one of the most important dates in the liturgical calendar and in some parts of the world today is celebrated as Christmas Day. On the surface, we celebrate the arrival of the magi—those earthly kings of wisdom who, by interpreting the night sky, are brought to pay homage to the baby Jesus with gold, frankincense and myrrh. As they approach the Christmas crib scene in church, the shepherds are still there, with sheep and oxen in constant adoration. Thus says the nativity play.

However, there is a deeper significance to the pastoral reverie that painters and carol writers put before us. Epiphany is about revealing God, revealed now as child-saviour, but also as anointed Messiah at his baptism in the Jordan (see Matthew 3) and as precociously wise in discussion with the elders in Jerusalem (see Luke 2:41–52). He is revealed as divine Word made human flesh in the opening verses of John's Gospel (John 1:1–18) and is then revealed as God's bringer of change and glory when he converts water into wine at Cana (John 2:1–11). Finally, on 2 February (Candlemas), we mark Christ's presentation in the Temple (see Luke 2:22–38).

This revealing of Christ in various ways puts into perspective our own earthly kingship (our dominion over the Earth), reminding us that we have a heavenly king who has bestowed on us whatever procreative power we have. Procreation means 'creation with God', not 'creation instead of God', and most parents have a sense of that, at least at first. God is to be praised not only for his creation revealed around us all the time, but also for his new creation revealed in Christ, at Epiphany and every day.

Prayer

*O God, our Lord, how wonderful is your revealing in the world! May all creation adore you now and always.
Amen*

GG

A safe stronghold

I will give thanks to the Lord with my whole heart; I will tell of all your wonderful deeds. I will be glad and exult in you; I will sing praise to your name, O Most High.... The Lord is a stronghold for the oppressed, a stronghold in times of trouble. And those who know your name put their trust in you, for you, O Lord, have not forsaken those who seek you.

The words of the opening of Psalm 9 are reminiscent of Psalm 46:1: 'God is our refuge and strength, a very present help in trouble'. Martin Luther based his great hymn, 'Ein Feste Burg' ('A safe stronghold our God is still'), on it, which echoes these words of Psalm 9 as well. We should not be surprised for, although each hymn or psalm is unique, there are certain common themes that emerge. God is often praised as creator, redeemer, helper, and here, protector (see also Psalm 84:9–11). It is only natural that, as a people who revere our creator God, we also look to him to sustain us in safety.

In the psalmist's day, protection was seen in battle terms, and some hymns have preserved the kind of language that describes God as strength and shield ('Guide me O thou great redeemer', for example). In the New Testament, though, we not only know of the saving work of Christ, but also of the sending of the Holy Spirit, as comforter and protector. The stronghold God identified by the psalmist is realized in the continuing presence of the Holy Spirit. At the Last Supper, Jesus specifically asked God to protect his disciples: 'Holy Father, protect them in your name that you have given me, so that they may be one, as we are one. While I was with them, I protected them in your name that you have given me… I ask you to protect them from the evil one' (John 17:11–12, 15).

Thus, for us, this psalm takes on a new meaning and direction after the coming of Christ. As Christians, we have the added gift of the Holy Spirit, through whom God continues to protect and comfort all who seek and put their trust in him.

Prayer

Heavenly Father, by your life-giving Spirit, guide and protect us in the way of Christ. Amen

GG

Stand-offish God?

Why, O Lord, do you stand far off? Why do you hide yourself in times of trouble? ... In the pride of their countenance the wicked say, 'God will not seek it out'; all their thoughts are, 'There is no God.' ... Why do the wicked renounce God, and say in their hearts, 'You will not call us to account'? ... O Lord, you will hear the desire of the meek; you will strengthen their heart, you will incline your ear to do justice for the orphan and the oppressed, so that those from earth may strike terror no more.

All too often we hear the question, 'Why does a loving God allow suffering?' and it is with this question that this psalm opens. While good people suffer, the wicked take advantage of God's apparent disinterest. The psalmist says that they exploit the poor and needy because they believe that the weak have no one to defend them. The logic works like this: there is no evidence for the existence of God, therefore there is no God and, even if people call on him in defence, they are wasting their time, and while they are doing so they can be further exploited.

The psalmist rails against this cynical reasoning and so can we! The news frequently contains stories of people being abused at every level—children, the sick, the elderly and, more widely, ethnic groups and faith communities. We might even feel that sometimes Christianity is picked on in this way. The Church is a cheap and easy target and the people of God have got used to it being so. Worse still, we now live in the shadow of those who would 'strike terror' on Earth, who feel no remorse for the damage they do to people, property and livelihoods, and for some it is all in the name of God!

Good people have always been vulnerable. Christ made himself vulnerable and was ridiculed, tortured, humiliated and judicially murdered because he was good and stood up for those who had no other defender. In his resurrection, we are reminded that we have a God who cares for all of us and knows exactly what it is like to be abused by those who know no better.

Sunday reflection

When did someone last ridicule your beliefs? What did you do about it?

GG

How long, O Lord?

How long, O Lord? Will you forget me forever? How long will you hide your face from me? How long must I bear pain in my soul, and have sorrow in my heart all day long? How long shall my enemy be exalted over me? ... But I trusted in your steadfast love; my heart shall rejoice in your salvation. I will sing to the Lord, because he has dealt bountifully with me.

As in Psalm 10 yesterday, we begin with a cry to an inaccessible God who appears to have let his servant down, yet within a few verses we have an acknowledgement that this is only how it feels, not how it really is. Here are words of hope for any who feel abandoned for, although it felt like this for the psalmist, he concludes by revealing that his despondency turned to confidence when he trusted in God's steadfast love.

What we may learn here is that what we feel about God often reveals more about us than it does about God. It is not that God is inscrutable and inaccessible, but that when we are down, we may create a distance between us and God. God does not make himself inaccessible to us; rather, we make it so. Sin and doubt and fear get in the way, but trust in God blows the clouds of doubt and fear away, making visible all the good things God does for, with and to us.

There is something about human existence that tends towards gloom and doom rather than light and joy. It is so easy to become clouded by such an instinct. God wants us to be people who are positive, loving, singing, joyful. While circumstances affect us, giving us grief and pain, this is not the will of God. God's will is that, in all things, we should turn to him, trust in him and enjoy the benefits of the salvation revealed to us and brought to us in Christ.

The question is not, 'How long O Lord will you forget me?' but 'How long O Lord will you love me?' And the answer, of course, is forever.

Prayer

Remove the clouds of doubt and fear, O Lord, so that we may see and love you as you really are. Amen

GG

No, not one!

Fools say in their hearts, 'There is no God.' They are corrupt, they do abominable deeds; there is no one who does good. The Lord looks down from heaven on humankind to see if there are any who are wise, who seek after God. They have all gone astray, they are all alike perverse; there is no one who does good, no, not one.... O that deliverance for Israel would come from Zion! When the Lord restores the fortunes of his people, Jacob will rejoice; Israel will be glad.

Now the psalmist is upset, so upset that he is making one of those generalizations that we still hear today: 'No one loves me', 'everyone is bad'. Can it be true that there is *no one* who is good?

On one level it can be. Remember the Pharisee calling Jesus 'good', and Jesus replying 'Why do you call me good? No one is good but God alone' (Luke 18:18). True goodness is not to be found in fallen humanity, but only in God, to whom Christ leads us.

There seems to be another, relative sense of goodness, which is still very much referred to these days. Goodness and faith are well and truly separate in the modern mind and the former is the more highly valued. The problem is, what is goodness without a framework of faith? If absolute goodness is unavailable to us, by what standard can we measure goodness if we leave God out of the equation?

It is certainly foolish to speak of good people if we do not know what goodness really is. It is foolish to deny the existence of God, because he provides the ultimate standard and purpose for goodness. No wonder the despondent psalmist believes that there isn't anyone good! For him, like us, the standard of goodness comes from God, whom he characterizes as looking down from above. In Christ we have a God who walked among us, victim of those who foolishly denounced goodness and deliverer of all who suffer from the evil of others. It is true that there is not a single person alive who is good, but as a result of the foolishness of the cross, goodness becomes accessible again in Christ.

Prayer

In you, O Lord, we rejoice and are glad, for in you goodness and truth have dwelt among us. Amen

GG

We shall never be moved

O Lord, who may abide in your tent?... Those who walk blamelessly, and do what is right... who do not slander with their tongue, and do no evil to their friends, nor take up a reproach against their neighbours; in whose eyes the wicked are despised, but who honour those who fear the Lord; who stand by their oath even to their hurt; who do not lend money at interest, and do not take a bribe against the innocent. Those who do these things shall never be moved.

Some people have difficulty distinguishing between the proper use of 'will' and 'shall'. Students of grammar are told of a drowning swimmer who calls out: 'I *will* be drowned, and no one *shall* save me!'. He is left to his fate because no one pays any attention, as the swimmer's tragic misuse of the English language implies that he wants to drown! Swap the words round and it means something quite different.

'Shall' is used in most translations of this psalm. The virtuous shall not fall or be moved. The psalmist lists dubious activities to be avoided, thus leading to Godly security and safety. Evildoers, though, shall not be secure in their position. Here again we have a promise of justice for the just and downfall for the unjust.

We are reminded of the famous song 'We shall not be moved'. Written in 1931, it makes the linguistic mistake that is so crucial for the psalm from which it drew its inspiration. 'Shall' expresses a simple future—'I shall go shopping tomorrow'—but the word 'will' expresses a wilful determination—'I will not give in.'

Nowadays the distinction between these two is blurred, but the psalmist is not referring to the rebellious resistance that the song conveys. The psalm is much more matter-of-fact. If we act justly, it is a simple conclusion that God will stand by us. The psalmist is not mincing words, nor presenting some complicated ethical consequence of good behaviour or righteous action. Rather, he is saying, 'Do the right thing, and you'll be OK.' Sometimes it really is as simple as that and no complexity of language or usage can disguise or alter it. Those who walk blamelessly shall never be moved.

Prayer

God of justice, keep us immovable as we walk in your way of righteousness. Amen

GG

The path of life

I keep the Lord always before me; because he is at my right hand, I shall not be moved. Therefore my heart is glad, and my soul rejoices; my body also rests secure. For you do not give me up to Sheol, or let your faithful one see the Pit. You show me the path of life. In your presence there is fullness of joy; in your right hand are pleasures for evermore.

Part of this psalm is sometimes read as a coffin is brought into a funeral. These ancient words comfort mourners and they also gave hope and solace to people long before Christ came and opened the gates to everlasting life. Sheol is not best associated with 'hell', but with 'the place of the dead'—a more neutral place than any location of grotesque punishment. The psalmist expresses his gratitude that God has delivered and given him good prospects for the future, but in the light of Christ we find a more inspiring perspective. Peter quotes this psalm when preaching, reminding his hearers that although David, the psalmist, died and was buried, his words indicate the resurrection of the Messiah (Acts 2:25–33). Paul also makes this connection in Acts 13:35: 'You will not let your Holy One experience corruption.'

Put like this, we might be able to hear the echoes of Handel's *Messiah*: 'Thou didst not leave his soul in hell', which has been a crucial devotional aid since its first performance in 1742. Before the coming of Christ, Psalm 16 was expressive of short-term hope, with perhaps a hint of future vision for a day when death would lose its sting (1 Corinthians 15:55–56), but after the resurrection it becomes a clue to Christ, buried in the Old Testament, for all to discover and draw comfort from.

Whether we see this psalm as comforting to Christians who die, promising eternal life or we prefer, with Peter and Paul, to see references to Jesus, his resurrection is a precursor to our own. Where he has gone we may go too (John 14:3) and so the two visions come together, revealing a deeper meaning and purpose for all who turn to him. Psalm 16 is about eternal life, before its time.

Prayer

Do not abandon us to death, O Lord, but lead us to your right hand on high. Amen

GG

The Lord is my rock

I love you, O Lord, my strength. The Lord is my rock, my fortress, and my deliverer, my God, my rock in whom I take refuge, my shield, and the horn of my salvation, my stronghold. I call upon the Lord, who is worthy to be praised; so I shall be saved from my enemies…. The Lord lives! Blessed be my rock, and exalted be the God of my salvation. For this I will extol you, O Lord, among the nations, and sing praises to your name.

When we think of God as our 'rock', we might think of the lovely old hymn 'Rock of ages, cleft for me' or we might recall Jesus saying to Peter 'on this rock I will build my church' (Matthew 16:18). Here, however, God is the rock—the ancient, immovable, solid, strong pillar of shelter. Picture a grey, craggy outcrop on a wind-swept English landscape or a sand-coloured boulder in the midst of a barren desert. Such a rock can protect a traveller from ravaging storms of rain or sand.

Rocks are part of the fabric of the landscape, and not only on our world. Where there is no life, no water, nor even light, there are rocks, hurtling through the universe or scattered on lonely planets far away. The Earth on which we live is made up of various kinds of rock, some of which collided with this planet millions of years ago. To describe God as a rock is to remind ourselves that he existed even before the world began.

Rocks are the oldest things we can conceive and God is older, greater and stronger than they. To be able to take refuge in him is to relate to the beginnings of history and the farthest reaches of the cosmos. We can also remember that Jesus is 'the firstborn of all creation; for in him all things in heaven and on earth were created' (Colossians 1:15–16). Our planet, therefore, is not simply the 'third rock from the Sun', as a sci-fi sitcom calls it, but is the creator's beloved location of salvation, where the redeemer of the world and all creation was born—Jesus Christ our Lord.

Prayer

God we praise you, rock of all ages, saviour of the universe. Amen

GG

Creation tells

The heavens are telling the glory of God; and the firmament proclaims his handiwork. Day to day pours forth speech, and night to night declares knowledge. There is no speech, nor are there words; their voice is not heard; yet their voice goes out through all the earth, and their words to the end of the world.

You may recognize these words as the text that Joseph Haydn used to complete the first part of his oratorio *The Creation*. It is a joyful proclamation that sums up the wonder of the creation, God's satisfaction in it and our delight in it. The version of Psalm 19 that Haydn used was actually written by the great poet John Milton, who put it into the mouths of the angels Raphael, Gabriel and Uriel. This dramatized approach is not only very engaging and effective, but is also a bit like the kind of dramatized reading that many churches are now rediscovering. It is nothing new, of course—we can trace dramatization of the Bible back to medieval mystery plays and beyond.

Behind it all there is the greater drama—that of creation, which is what the psalmist is writing about. Creation, he says, praises God and the mere passage of time tells us something of God's creative love. Our simple ability to recognize the hand of God in the world around us speaks volumes about creation and our place in the midst of it. We are not only created beings, but, uniquely, we have the ability to observe and understand that we are. The created order cannot articulate itself in words, but through it God's voice is proclaimed everywhere. This is, in effect, what philosophers call the 'argument from design', which is that we can say that God exists because all around us we see his handiwork. It is a powerful and persuasive claim.

The psalmist was on to this idea many centuries ago, identifying drama in natural wonder, which communicates God's glory without a word of language. Even today, we might still say, who needs words when we have the Word himself, revealed in the beauty of the Earth and in the incarnate Word-made-flesh, Jesus Christ?

Prayer

God, you are revealed in earth and sky, in words and Word: we adore you in Jesus Christ, your Son our Lord. Amen

GG

MARK 5:4–13 (CEV, ABRIDGED)

Power over demons

No one could control him [the man with an evil spirit]. Night and day he was in the graveyard or on the hills, yelling and cutting himself with stones… He shouted, 'Jesus, Son of God in heaven, what do you want with me? Promise me in God's name that you won't torture me!' … Jesus asked, 'What is your name?' The man answered, 'My name is Lots, because I have "lots" of evil spirits'… Jesus let them [the spirits] go, and they went out of the man and into the pigs. The whole herd… rushed down the steep bank into the lake and drowned

Jesus has just stilled a storm. Now he encounters a storm of demons. Mark gives us a vivid picture of their victim's pitiful state, living among tombs cut into rocky hillsides, the haunt of wild animals and the truly destitute, all classed as unclean. The man is emaciated from lack of food and sleep. He has no rest. Demonic strength loosens his fetters (vv. 3–4), but binds him tightly to the powers of darkness. He is a fearsome sight, but Jesus encounters him calmly, with great compassion.

Then follows a battle as intense as the wildest storm. The power of the Son of God defeats demonic legions.

The demons want to stay in the place of death. Luke 11:24–26 tells how spirits return to torment their victims. When the USSR was freed from the stranglehold of communism, chaos followed as many dark forces swept in. Those involved in deliverance ministry will know that the person exorcized should always pray to be filled with the Holy Spirit.

Some people worry about the fate of the pigs. So did their owners! The drowning of unclean pigs is a convincing demonstration of Jesus' words in Mark 3:27: the strong man, Satan, is bound and Jesus is snatching his property—the mind of a man—from the enemy whose defeat was prophesied when evil spirits wailed, 'Have you come to destroy us?' (Mark 1:24). The answer is 'Yes!' Like so much in Mark's Gospel, this incident looks forward to the victory of the cross.

Jesus still destroys demons and restores outcasts. We pray in his name for those who are preyed on by dark forces.

Sunday prayer

Strong deliverer, come. Set poor captives free and fill dark places with your light.

JR

MARK 5:14–20 (CEV, ABRIDGED)

Clothed and in his right mind

Then the people came out to see what had happened. When they came to Jesus, they saw the man who had once been full of demons... sitting there with his clothes on and in his right mind, and they were terrified... [They] started begging Jesus to leave... the man begged to go with him. But Jesus... said, 'Go home to your family and tell them how much the Lord has done for you and how good he has been to you.'

People from the farms and villages nearby rush out to the place of tombs. Instead of some sort of supernatural wonderworker, they find something even more amazing—a sight as tranquil as a lake when the day is calm. The man they knew to have been demon-possessed (perhaps some of them had locked chains around him) is sitting beside Jesus, 'clothed and in his right mind' (KJV). We all have our favourite Bible verses and this is one of mine. It's so normal, so human and so very beautiful. We're not told where the clothes came from. Perhaps the disciples (not mentioned here) shared their clothes. Perhaps Jesus covered the man with his own robe.

The terrified villagers can't take it in. It's too much—the dramatic rush of 2000 pigs into the lake. They're too frightened to notice the quiet normality of two men enjoying each other's company. They beg Jesus to leave. Jesus complies. The man wants to follow the Lord who has treated him with compassion and restored him to his humanity, but Jesus, wise counsellor, says with the modesty and common sense we will meet again later this week, 'Go home to your family and tell them how much the Lord has done for you and how good he has been to you.'

It is said so simply. It would be quite an ego trip to follow a wonderworker. It would boost the man's confidence and make him feel safe, but the normal responsibilities of daily life matter to Jesus. The man obeys and spreads the good news of deliverance far and wide in Gentile territory.

Prayer

Lord, bring your loving presence into the events that make up our day. When we are distracted or upset, let us pause to talk with you and then others around us will know how good you are to us.

JR

Power over disease

Jairus... knelt at Jesus' feet and started begging him for help. He said, 'My daughter is about to die! Please come and touch her, so she will get well and live.' ... In the crowd was a woman who had been bleeding for twelve years... She had said to herself, 'If I can just touch his [Jesus'] clothes, I will get well.' As soon as she touched them, her bleeding stopped, and she knew she was well... Jesus felt power go out from him... and asked, 'Who touched my clothes?'

Desperate situations demand desperate actions. In the crowd, as desperate as the anguished father, was a woman who didn't dare approach Jesus openly. As a Sunday school teacher and writer of children's Bible stories, I know only too well the difficulty in explaining this awkward intrusion into the restoration of a little girl. You can't miss it out—the whole drama depends on it.

Studying this chapter, I realized what a masterpiece the whole of Mark's Gospel is. The characters and settings leap vividly from the page. Incidents balance each other. Today's healing is the mirror image of tomorrow's, when a twelve-year-old girl is restored to life. In terms of the Law, the woman is a complete outcast and she has been 'dead' in that sense for twelve years (Leviticus 15:25–31). She can no longer wash or cook for her family, worship with them or eat with them. In Thursday's reading, at the child's deathbed, Jesus will do the touching, but today he is the one who is touched. He will draw a veil of silence over the little girl's recovery. Today he demands a public confession.

Jairus' faith is stretched to breaking point. He has gone to such lengths to save his daughter and every moment counts, but Jesus allows an unclean woman to cause this dreadful delay. He knows the cost of the woman's healing—and its consequence. He questions her publicly so that her restoration will be authenticated in the eyes of her family and society as a whole.

Reflection

Not 'magic' but faith; not control but relationship. Jesus points away from himself, praising the woman's faith, calling her 'daughter' (v. 34, NRSV). We belong to this healing relationship, too. Hear Jesus call you by name, 'my daughter' or 'my son'.

JR

Power over panic

While Jesus was still speaking, some men came from Jairus' home and said, 'Your daughter has died! Why bother the teacher any more?' Jesus heard what they said, and he said to Jairus, 'Don't worry. Just have faith!' Jesus... Peter and the two brothers, James and John... went home with Jairus and saw the people crying and making a lot of noise. Then Jesus went inside and said... 'Why are you crying and carrying on like this? The child isn't dead. She is just asleep.' But the people laughed at him.

The delay caused by the woman seemed to have had the worst possible outcome for Jairus. Perhaps he wished he hadn't 'bothered' Jesus in the first place. He'd done Jesus quite a favour, publicly humbling himself before the controversial young rabbi. He hadn't even objected when he had been pushed aside by the needs of the interfering woman. And now, when the thing he most dreaded had happened, Jesus says calmly, 'Don't worry. Just have faith'!

Isn't it the same with us? We trust Jesus. Like Jairus, we're not ashamed to bring our needs to him and beg for his help... but then things go wrong. Instead of rushing to put them right, he says, 'Don't worry.' Don't worry?!

When that happens, think of Jairus—the man of means and influence reduced to a state of total need and helplessness. His hopes are shattered, but he's still holding on, and Jesus, who hadn't rejected his desperate prayer, is still walking home with him. Jairus knows Jesus isn't mocking him. There is love in this teacher's voice and also, surely, an encouraging smile. So Jairus sticks by Jesus in spite of the sneering tone of the messengers' remarks and the jeers of the mourners.

Jesus, who drove out hosts of demons and healed a woman whose suffering had gone on far too long, has power over panic, too. Far from being intimidated by the hired mourners with their noisy show of grief, he challenges them with the simplicity of perfect faith: 'The child isn't dead. She is just asleep.'

Jairus doesn't join in with the mocking laughter. He follows Jesus to his daughter's room (v. 40).

Prayer

Lord, when we panic, remind us that you are at our side. When we worry, encourage us. We know that you love us. Let us sense your smile.

JR

Power over death

After Jesus had sent them all out of the house, he took the girl's father and mother and his three disciples and went to where she was. He took the twelve-year-old girl by the hand and said, 'Talitha, koum!' which means 'Little girl, get up!' The girl got straight up and started walking around. Everyone was greatly surprised. But Jesus ordered them not to tell anyone what had happened. Then he said, 'Give her something to eat.'

Our readings this week began in the place of tombs. Now we enter a room in a rich man's house. In contrast to the clamour and crush of the crowd and the loud crying of the hired mourners, a great stillness surrounds the twelve-year-old girl. Yet death has made her as unclean as the woman who has been an outcast for twelve years and the demon-possessed man. Once again, Jesus defies defilement—he takes the girl's hand. As he speaks to her, we hear the cadences of Aramaic, his mother tongue. The keynote is simplicity. There is nothing remarkable about waking a child from sleep. Once again, Jesus refuses the role of a powerful miracle worker and once again we sense his smile as he tells the startled parents that their daughter needs some breakfast after so long and deep a sleep.

There is a mystery contained in this story, too. *Talitha* also means 'lamb' and *koum* can be translated as 'rise!' At the dawning of the third day, the power of death will be defeated and the Lamb will arise. He will break bread, eat fish and cook breakfast on the lakeshore. All the normal things of everyday life will have a new perspective—and this is the wonder of the gospel, envisioned here in the outstretched hand of an elder brother arousing a little sister who has overslept.

Contemplate this icon of our gospel faith. We see the young girl stirring from sleep. She feels the touch of Jesus' hand, hears his voice and opens her eyes to see his face. One day we, too, will be aroused from the sleep the world calls death. The Lord will take us by the hand. We will hear his voice and see his face.

Prayer

We praise you…. You overcame the sting of death and opened the kingdom of heaven to all believers.

Te Deum Laudamus, *Common Worship*

JR

Familiarity breeds contempt

Jesus left and returned to his home town... The next Sabbath he taught in the Jewish meeting place. Many of the people who heard him were amazed and asked, 'How can he do all this...? Isn't he the carpenter, the son of Mary? Aren't James, Joseph, Judas, and Simon his brothers? Don't his sisters still live here in our town?' ... Jesus could not perform any miracles there, except to heal a few sick people... He was surprised that the people did not have any faith.

The Gospels show us clearly how Jesus values the simple things in everyday life, but he also transforms them with his presence. No one is a no-hoper. We see the glory of God in broken bread and glimpse his splendour in wild flowers. The people of Nazareth, who had watched Jesus grow up, couldn't see beyond the local lad at the carpenter's bench, so they missed out on the miracle.

Their comments give us a glimpse into Jesus' birth family. Joseph isn't named, so early commentators on scripture presumed he was dead, giving rise to the tradition that Joseph was an old man when he married Mary. This is a controversial passage for some Christians. The Eastern Orthodox and Roman Catholic Churches explain the brothers and sisters of Jesus either as Joseph's children before he married Mary or else as cousins. Other Christians believe that these were the children of both Mary and Joseph, born after Jesus.

Whatever the case, the sad thing is that his closest family don't believe in him. Later, though, Mary will stand with him at the cross (John 19:25–27). She will be gathered into the faith-family of the Church, and so will his brothers (Acts 1:14). Brother James will become a leader of the church in Jerusalem (Acts 12:17; 15:13).

Thus, there is a note of sadness here. We've seen demons subdued, a hopeless woman restored to full participation in her community and death defeated. Now, among his own townspeople, Jesus feels dishonoured and could only help a few sick people. How would it be, I wonder, if Jesus visited your church or mine next Sunday? Would he be surprised by our lack of faith?

Reflection

Familiarity often breeds contempt. Do our worship and daily prayer honour the Lord and enable him to release his healing power?

JR

MARK 6:7–12 (CEV, ABRIDGED)

Travelling light

Then he [Jesus] called together his twelve apostles and sent them out two by two with power over evil spirits. He told them, '… don't carry food or a travelling bag or any money… don't take along a change of clothes…. If any place won't welcome you or listen to your message, leave and shake the dust from your feet as a warning to them.' The apostles left and started telling everyone to turn to God. They forced out many demons and healed a lot of sick people by putting olive oil on them.

Jesus had many disciples, but only twelve apostles—chosen as his closest companions to preach and drive out demons with him. Off they go, travelling light, commissioned by Jesus to turn people to God, heal the sick and defeat demonic forces. This is still the mission of the Church, but we have lost that original simplicity and urgency. Our secular world has rational explanations for illness and disaster and so we diminish the demons and forget the healing oil. The warning about shaking dust from the feet when leaving an unwelcoming place falls hard on many ears today.

Unlike other itinerant preachers who lived by begging favours, Jesus' apostles were on a mission for God, who meets our needs without a begging bowl. The apostles were also to take out to the world the holiness associated with temple worship and sacrifice. Contemporary documents reveal that men could not enter the temple with a wallet or with dusty feet. This episode points to the cross when Jesus, the sinless one, becomes the sacrifice for sin. Temple ritual will become obsolete, while everyday life is hallowed because God Almighty has entered the world in human form.

A young man once took Jesus at his word and followed these commands literally. The only son of a rich businessman, a well-known partygoer and late-night reveller, he began to live and preach the poverty of Jesus. When he heard these verses read aloud, he threw away his spare clothing and his wallet and travelled light to live out the gospel of love. His name was Francis, later known as Francis of Assisi.

Prayer

Lord Jesus, give me eyes of faith to look beyond my daily cares and an obedient heart to carry out your commands.

JR

MARK 6:21–29 (CEV, ABRIDGED)

The death of John the Baptist

Herod gave a great birthday celebration… The daughter of Herodias came in and danced for Herod and his guests. She pleased them so much that Herod said, 'Ask for anything, and it's yours!' … The girl left and asked her mother, 'What do you think I should ask for?' Her mother answered, 'The head of John the Baptist!' … The king… ordered a guard to cut off John's head there in prison. The guard put the head on a dish and took it to the girl. Then she gave it to her mother. When John's followers learnt that he had been killed, they took his body and put it in a tomb.

Jesus was born into a world of violence and danger. Herod the Great wanted to murder him. His superstitious son, Herod Antipas, was clearly bothered about the beheading of John (vv. 16, 20, 26). Attracted to righteousness, he might have been a better ruler, but he was too weak. His wife, Herodias, operating through her daughter, had her will.

John's life was consistent with his preaching. He boldly condemned Herod's incestuous marriage (vv. 17–18) and so John, who had slept beneath the stars, was shut in a dark dungeon. Herod 'knew that John was a good and holy man' (v. 20), but he preferred to execute him than lose face in front of his birthday guests. John paid the highest price for his testimony.

This is the only episode in Mark's Gospel in which Jesus is not on stage, but the scene points to the Lord's death at the hands of self-serving political rulers, as well as his resurrection. Mark writes that John's disciples laid his body in a tomb—but Jesus will rise again.

There are still Christians who pay the highest price for following Jesus. Those who suffer for their faith are vibrant witnesses that resurrection life means more than personal safety. On trial for her faith in the USSR in 1964, 24-year-old Aida Skripnikova rightly pointed out that persecutors are usually remembered negatively. The sorry episode in Herod's court shows him as a weakling while John's witness rings true to the end.

Sunday prayer

Father, as we gather to worship, we pray for Christians persecuted for their faith, those who dare not worship openly and those on missions to closed and dangerous lands.

JR

Resources in a desert place

Jesus said [to the disciples], 'Let's go to a place where we can be alone and get some rest.' They left in a boat.... But many people saw them leave and worked out where they were going. So people from every town ran on ahead and got there first. When Jesus... saw the large crowd.... He felt sorry for the people and started teaching them many things. That evening the disciples came to Jesus and said, '... Let the crowds leave, so they can... buy something to eat.' Jesus replied, 'You give them something to eat.'... They... answered, 'We have five small loaves of bread and two fish.'

This story was very important for the early Church. It's the only miracle to be recounted in all four Gospels. The loaves and fish are depicted on very early Christian mosaics—another sign of the importance placed on this story. There's a subtext from the Old Testament at work here, as is so often the case in the Gospels. Exodus 16:1–18 tells how the people of Israel complained to Moses that they were so hungry they wanted to return to Egypt. The Lord heard their complaints and sent flocks of quails in the evening, and heaven-sent 'bread' in the morning. The God-given feast in a desert place is repeated when Jesus feeds this large crowd from such small supplies of food.

Jesus and the apostles had been trying to get away to rest and debrief after their mission and the disturbing murder of Jesus' cousin, John (vv. 31–34), but people saw them leaving and raced ahead along the shore. Jesus set aside his own wishes to respond to their need.

After years of living in a clergy home, I often groan when the phone goes at mealtimes. It doesn't matter what time the meal is happening, it always seems to ring just then! The disciples were put out, too—our resources only stretch so far—but Jesus sees beyond our irritation. The people are like sheep without a shepherd (v. 34). Jesus, the Good Shepherd, rescues his flock from the briars of ignorance, teaching them the scriptures and nourishing them with small human resources, bread and fish, multiplied by his God-given power.

Prayer

Lord, shepherd me to green pastures and, when my resources are low, please fill me and feed me.

JR

Struggling against the wind

Straight away, Jesus made his disciples get into the boat and start back across to Bethsaida. But… went up on the side of a mountain to pray…. Later that evening… the boat was somewhere in the middle of the lake. He [Jesus] could see that the disciples were struggling hard, because they were rowing against the wind. Not long before morning Jesus came towards them… walking on the water…. All of them [the disciples] saw him and were terrified. But… he said, 'Don't worry! I am Jesus. Don't be afraid.' He then got into the boat with them, and the wind died down. The disciples were completely confused.

In our readings, we've seen that Jesus often uses everyday life to reveal God's glory, but today we see him in another light. There is nothing normal or everyday about a man walking through the darkness over choppy waves against a wild wind. No wonder the disciples are terrified and confused! They're struggling against the wind, but they are not in danger and, indeed, Jesus seems to be about to pass by (v. 48). What is happening here?

Once again, the Old Testament comes to our aid. The clue is in verse 52: 'they could not understand the true meaning of the loaves of bread'. Yesterday we saw that the feeding of the 5000 runs in tandem with the miracle of manna in the desert. Moses, who fed the people, also stretched his arm over the sea and God parted the water (Exodus 14:21–22). Now Jesus, who fed a multitude, actually walks on the water. Mark's Gospel offers a collage of icons depicting him as Son of God and this episode is one of them. 'God alone… stepped on the sea,' says Job (9:8), while Psalm 77 adds, 'You walked through the water of the mighty sea, but your footprints were never seen' (v. 19). Either we believe and cry 'my Lord and my God' (John 20:28) or, like the disciples, struggling against the wind, are troubled and confused.

Jesus, though, does not pass us by—he gets into the boat of our lives. The wind dies, dawn breaks and we arrive at the shore, with him.

Prayer

Just as I am, though tossed about with many a conflict, many a doubt… I come.

Charlotte Elliott (1789–1871)

JR

Rules and true piety

In every village or farm or marketplace where Jesus went, the people brought their sick to him. They begged him to let them just touch his clothes, and everyone who did was healed. Some Pharisees and several teachers of the Law of Moses from Jerusalem came and gathered around Jesus. They noticed that some of his disciples ate without first washing their hands…. The Pharisees and teachers asked Jesus, 'Why don't your disciples obey what our ancestors taught us to do? Why do they eat without washing their hands?' Jesus replied, '… You disobey God's commands in order to obey what humans have taught…. Didn't Moses command you to respect your father and mother?… But you let people get by without helping their parents when they should.'

The issue seemed to be ritual hand-washing, but the big issue is one the apostle Paul (whose feast is commemorated today) wrestled with: law and grace. Paul discovered that true freedom is found in Christ. Jesus warns that rigid obedience to 'the teachings of our ancestors' is really disobedience to God (vv. 8–9, 12). These 'teachings' were human traditions that put an ever more rigid interpretation on the first five books of the Old Testament. Jesus also speaks severely to those who put religiosity above the needs of their parents (v. 11). This is a challenge in an ageing society. Can churches, desperate to attract families and young people, include older people in meaningful ways in an all ages service? Can those who lead worship in residential homes do so in ways that speak with—and not at—older people?

Like the prophets before him, Jesus proclaims that the loving attitude he himself always showed towards the sick and needy pleases God more than strict observance of the Law. Turn to Isaiah 58 to see how God declares that acts of justice and mercy mean far more than religious observance.

However, Mark 6:56 shows how closely Jesus fulfilled at least one of the Law's requirements. The sick, who longed to touch his clothes, stretched their hands towards the tassels (not translated in CEV) worn at the edge of the outer garment by observant Jews (Deuteronomy 22:12).

Prayer

Lord, may we who love your word also love those who long to touch even the edges of your garments.

JR

Hearts and minds

Jesus called the crowd together again and said, 'Pay attention and try to understand. The food that you put into your mouth doesn't make you unclean and unfit to worship God. The bad words that come out of your mouth are what make you unclean.' [The disciples] asked him what these sayings meant… He said: What comes out of your heart is what makes you unclean. Out of your heart comes evil thoughts, vulgar deeds, stealing murder, unfaithfulness in marriage, greed, meanness, deceit, indecency, envy, insults, pride, and foolishness. All these come from your heart, and they are what make you unfit to worship God.

Jesus continues his teaching about right living. He tells the crowd that strict rules about food don't count in God's sight because the things we say matter more than what we eat. Afterwards he explains to the disciples that the real difficulty isn't diet, it's a sinful heart.

Food was a big issue for the first Christians. As Jesus' teachings began to spread to the Gentiles, Jewish Christians had to learn to eat food that they had previously considered unclean. What Jesus said on this matter, therefore, would have been very important for them. Later, a different problem arose concerning food on sale in the market that had been offered to idols in pagan temples. This problem still confronts Christians in multifaith situations such as in India where food at a family feast might first have been offered in the temple.

For us today, there are the issues of fair trade, fish farming and overfishing, battery hens and food additives. Huge conglomerates control the food we buy and the prices we pay. These are big problems and we often feel out of our depth, but Jesus confronts us with the real challenge. He lists twelve major faults. Some are obvious crimes, but what about greed, insults, pride and foolishness? God requires radical righteousness. Mercifully, he also provides a way out for us. When our heart has been put right by the sin-offering Jesus made on the cross, our minds respond more clearly to these other problems.

Prayer

Lord, thank you that you look deep into my heart and know my thoughts. Lead me in your ways. May those who govern nations use their power for good.

JR

Crumbs from the children's table

A woman whose daughter had an evil spirit in her heard where Jesus was. And straight away she came and knelt down at his feet. The woman was Greek... She begged Jesus to force the demon out of her daughter. But Jesus said, 'The children must first be fed! It isn't right to take away their food and feed it to dogs.' The woman replied, 'Lord, even dogs eat the crumbs that children drop from the table.' Jesus answered, 'That's true! You may go now. The demon has left your daughter.' When the woman got home she found her child lying on the bed. The demon had gone.

In today's startling story, Jesus refuses the woman's request because 'the children must be fed first'. The words refer to his mission to Israel—even though, as our two previous readings showed, the people of Israel had become bogged down in religious observance that hindered their openness to God.

In contrast, this Greek woman is so desperate that she won't be put off by Jesus' initial refusal. As a non-Jew, she may have come to Jesus because she had heard he was a wonder-worker and this might have been another reason for Jesus refusing to help her. However, she kneels at his feet, an attitude of worship. She is persistent and points out that 'even the dogs' deserve a crumb or two from the children's table. In other words, she acknowledges that the children are indeed being fed, for the Messiah is among them. Her faith impresses Jesus—and he heals her daughter.

This story is startling because Jesus allows this non-Jewish woman to let him change his mind. He dialogues with her. He engages with her person to person. We could even say that he discusses theology with her! This is cross-cultural interaction with a vengeance. It is an enormous encouragement for us when we pray for others. It teaches us to be focused and persistent, to hold on —and enjoy the dialogue, too.

Yes, but what about when healing doesn't come? This woman's faith encourages us to keep on asking, as Jesus teaches his disciples to do, and to believe that one day we too will go home to find that those crumbs have become an abundant feast.

Prayer

You are the same Lord whose nature is always to have mercy.

JR

MARK 7:32–37A (CEV, ABRIDGED)

Be opened!

Some people brought to him [Jesus] a man who was deaf and could hardly talk... After Jesus had taken him aside from the crowd, he stuck his fingers in the man's ears. Then he spat and put the spit on the man's tongue. Jesus looked up towards heaven, and with a groan, he said, 'Effatha!' which means 'Open up!' At once the man could hear, and he had no more trouble talking clearly... They [the people] were completely amazed and said, 'Everything he does is good!'

In the last two weeks, we have seen Jesus show his power over demons, disease and death itself, but the crowd, and even the disciples, fail to understand all that they have seen and heard. Here, Jesus' command, 'Be opened!' cures a man who is without hearing and almost mute. There is a spiritual truth here. Faith means that our ears are open to Jesus' words and our lips to his praise: 'Everything he does is good' (v. 37). This echoes the creation story in Genesis 1, which tells how everything that God has done is good. Mark's carefully chosen words highlight the truth that Jesus the Saviour is indeed the Son of God.

The healing process is unusually detailed. Jesus uses his fingers and spittle. He looks up in prayer, sighs deeply and utters a single command, given here in his own language and translated. We had another example of words in the Lord's own Aramaic language in

Mark 5:41: 'Talitha koum' I personally feel that it's a great privilege to have these words preserved for us. There's an intimacy about language that draws us close to one another. It's as though the Lord allows us to hear the tones of his voice, inviting us to participate in the Gospel story as insiders and close friends.

Languages open doors and build bridges. When I first visited Moscow, I knew almost no Russian, but, after learning the language, when I met the same people, it was amazing. They were the same faces, but now I knew what they were saying. The deaf man must have felt just as excited. The shapes people's mouths made now had meaning—and he could speak back! No wonder he rushed about telling everyone the good news.

Prayer

Open my ears to hear your word and my lips to praise your name.

JR

Who is Jesus?

Many Christians would be surprised that the question even needs to be asked. Jesus is the Messiah, the Son of God. In fact, in much Christian thinking (and especially the words of some worship songs) he *is* 'God'. A quick glance at the kind of hymnbook that lists hymns by subject will confirm that Christianity is a 'Jesus' religion. In *Hymns Ancient and Modern New Standard*, for instance, there are 22 hymns on the subject of God the Father (Creator, Ruler) but 33 about Jesus. The Holy Spirit, as usual, is the neglected member of the Trinity, with just eight hymns.

For many people—enquirers, doubters, lapsed Christians—however, this is *the* question to ask: who is he? They are not convinced that this Jewish man from first-century Galilee was in any sense divine or 'God'. If they were convinced, it would necessarily change their view not just of him but also of the Christian faith. If God was uniquely present in Jesus, spoke through him, worked his will in the world through him, then, quite simply, that would be the most important thing that had ever happened on our planet. God has spoken to us, shown us the truth, not in a book or a code of conduct but in a person, one of us.

For the next fortnight we shall be looking at New Testament passages that set out to answer that question. Of course the writers are not neutral observers—they already believed in Jesus as the Son of God—yet their witness is important. It is based on the testimony of those who actually saw the events they relate, heard the words of Jesus, watched his crucifixion and even, in some cases, met the risen Lord.

We may find, in the course of these readings, that we have our faith in the divine sonship of Jesus strengthened at the same time as we have to rethink some of the language we use about him. Perhaps, in any case, language doesn't matter when we are confronted with the ultimate mystery that John's Gospel spells out in its magnificent prologue (John 1:1–18, see 31 January). This is truth that we shall never be able fully to comprehend on Earth. For now, we can only employ the language of faith: 'We believe in one Lord, Jesus Christ, the only Son of God... of one being with the Father'.

David Winter

LUKE 1:30–33 (NRSV)

The Son of the Most High

The angel said to her, 'Do not be afraid, Mary, for you have found favour with God. And now, you will conceive in your womb and bear a son, and you will name him Jesus. He will be great, and will be called the Son of the Most High, and the Lord God will give to him the throne of his ancestor David. He will reign over the house of Jacob forever, and of his kingdom there will be no end.'

The first thing Luke told us about Joseph, who was engaged to Mary, was that he was 'of the house of David' (1:27). Now his fiancée learns that the baby she will bear will inherit the throne of his ancestor, David. In other words, she was to be the mother of the Messiah, the long-awaited inheritor of the glory and power of David's empire. That would have been a big enough shock on its own for a teenage girl to absorb, but Mary is told more: 'he will be called the Son of the Most High'.

What might Mary have understood by the phrase? Our reading is conditioned by nearly 2000 years of Christian interpretation. It is a central tenet of our faith that Jesus is the Son of God, but what could it have meant to a first-century Jewish woman? Even in this Gospel, Adam is titled 'son of God' (3:38), meaning simply that God alone was the source of his existence. 'Sons of God' is used to describe human beings made in the image of God (Genesis 6:2, 4) and in Job to describe what the NRSV calls 'heavenly beings' (Job 1:6). So the title was known, but here the angel seems to give it a very distinct meaning. This is no mere human, nor some indeterminate 'heavenly being', but a baby who will be conceived by the action of the Holy Spirit and will be holy in a unique way.

Already the evangelist is preparing his readers. This is to be no ordinary child, nor even an ordinary prophet. They must read on....

Sunday reflection

Mary may not have realized the full significance of the angel's words. It was only as events unfolded—perhaps most fully after the resurrection of Jesus—that she came to appreciate the true nature of her son.

DW

Emmanuel

An angel of the Lord appeared to [Joseph] in a dream and said, 'Joseph, son of David, do not be afraid to take Mary as your wife, for the child conceived in her is from the Holy Spirit. She will bear a son, and you are to name him Jesus, for he will save his people from their sins.' All this took place to fulfil what had been spoken by the Lord through the prophet: 'Look, the virgin shall conceive and bear a son, and they shall name him Emmanuel,' which means, 'God is with us.'

Joseph was planning to call off the engagement—a rather more drastic step then than now—but God had other plans for Joseph and Mary. He was to take her as his wife, knowing that the child she would bear would be the longed-for saviour, the new Yeshua (Joshua), which is the Hebrew version of 'Jesus'. Joshua led the people of Israel to new life in the Promised Land and so would this special Son.

The baby was born, and they did name him 'Jesus'—a very common name at the time. Presumably this was the name by which they addressed him as he grew up in Nazareth and by which his friends and close associates knew him. Yet the only recorded instance in the Gospels of someone addressing him as 'Jesus' is at his crucifixion. The thief on the cross, presumably seeing his name written on the accusation above his head, called out 'Jesus, remember me when you come into your kingdom' (Luke 23:42). There is a touching appropriateness about that—the Saviour on the cross, the sinner receiving forgiveness in his dying moments.

So Jesus—Saviour—is the name by which millions of people have known Jesus. The other name mentioned here—Emmanuel—is seldom used, except in hymns, and, so far as we can tell, no one during his lifetime actually called him by that name. The prophecy, however, intrigued Matthew—'God is with us' or possibly 'God is on our side'. He returned to the phrase at the very end of his Gospel, when the risen Jesus promised his followers, 'I am with you always' (28:20).

Reflection

The coming of Jesus tells us that God is 'with us', on our side…
Emmanuel.

DW

John 1:14, 16–18 (NRSV)

Close to the Father's heart

And the Word became flesh and lived among us, and we have seen his glory, the glory as of a father's only son, full of grace and truth.... From his fullness we have all received, grace upon grace. The law indeed was given through Moses; grace and truth came through Jesus Christ. No one has ever seen God. It is God the only Son, who is close to the Father's heart, who has made him known.

Many people have asked and still ask, 'Does God exist? Where is he? What is he like? What (if anything) does he do?' At Jesus' last meal with his friends, one of the disciples, Philip, put it very starkly: 'Show us the Father, and we will be satisfied' (John 14:8). You bet they would! No more wondering whether or not to believe in God—they would have actually seen him!

Jesus' answer then is almost a paraphrase of the end of today's reading: 'Whoever has seen me has seen the Father' (14:9). If we want to know what God is 'like', look at his Son. In our reading the idea is expanded. The Word (Jesus) had the glory of 'a father's only son': 'like father, like son,' we say. This filial likeness goes much deeper than looks. This son is not only like his Father, but is 'close to his heart' (other translations say 'in the bosom of the Father'). It is from this uniquely intimate relationship that Jesus can reveal to human beings the very nature of God.

God made himself known in Jesus. What Jesus does mirrors what the Father does. Only a son could so perfectly unveil the nature of his father—and only a son who is 'close to his heart' shares his thoughts and intentions.

On that basis, what is God like? God is powerful, but also vulnerable, able to 'sympathize with our weaknesses' (Hebrews 4:15); the embodiment of mercy, love and forgiveness, with an open heart to all. One who was himself wounded and yet healed others. One who has conquered our two greatest enemies, evil and death.

Reflection

At Bethlehem, in a stable, God made himself known to us in a daring act of self-exposure. To those who received the Saviour he gave 'power to become children of God' (John 1:12).

DW

My Son, my Beloved

In those days Jesus came from Nazareth of Galilee and was baptized by John in the Jordan. And just as he was coming up out of the water, he saw the heavens torn apart and the Spirit descending like a dove on him. And a voice came from heaven, 'You are my Son, the Beloved; with you I am well pleased.'

John the Baptist was a highly significant figure in first-century Judaism. Indeed, he gets as much attention as Jesus from the Jewish historian Josephus. He stood in a succession of apocalyptic preachers during dark days for Israel—unless the nation repented and returned to the whole-hearted service of God, they were doomed. If they did, blessing would follow and the longed-for Saviour/Messiah would come. Crowds flocked to hear him, anxious for any sign that a new era of hope might be at hand.

Jesus—who, according to Luke, was a relative of John's—came to the Jordan to be baptized, along with thousands of others. However, this baptism was different. As he emerged from the water, he (Jesus… or John?) saw 'heaven torn apart' and the Spirit descending on him. The phrase 'like a dove' is interesting. Luke amplifies on it a little: 'in bodily form' (3:22) like a dove—something was visible, coming down to Jesus with the gentleness of a dove alighting on the ground. There was also a heavenly voice bearing testimony to the identity of this unique candidate for John's baptism: 'You are my Son, the Beloved'. This voice would be heard again at the transfiguration and later speaking of his 'glorification' through death (John 12:28).

There is an echo in the title 'Beloved' of the story of Abraham and Isaac, where the patriarch is called to offer his son—'your only son Isaac, whom you love' (Genesis 22:2)—as a sacrifice to God. It is interesting that in Islamic teaching, Jesus is entitled the 'Beloved Prophet'—though for Christians, of course, he is rather more: the Beloved Son.

Reflection

'For God so loved the world that he gave his only Son', John tells us (3:16). We also learn here that God loved his Son, his 'Beloved'. The whole message of our salvation is wrapped up in the arms of love— God's for his dear Son, and also for our fallen and rebellious race.

DW

Thursday 2 February

LUKE 2:29–32 (NRSV)

A light for the nations

'Master, now you are dismissing your servant in peace, according to your word; for my eyes have seen your salvation, which you have prepared in the presence of all peoples, a light for revelation to the Gentiles and for glory to your people Israel.'

Today is Candlemas, which, from as long ago as the fourth century, has marked the presentation of the infant Jesus in the temple 40 days after his birth. Through the centuries a procession with lighted candles has been a distinctive feature of the observance—hence, presumably, its name.

From a biblical point of view, candles seem appropriate because it was on that occasion in the temple that the aged Simeon described the child as 'a light for revelation', both to the people of Israel and, more prophetically, to the Gentiles (literally, the *ethnoi*, the 'nations'). The theme of light runs like a thread through the New Testament. The incarnate Word, made flesh in Jesus, would be a 'light for all people' (John 1:4). Jesus called himself 'the light of the world' (John 9:5), though in Matthew's Gospel, in the Sermon on the Mount, Jesus tells his disciples that they are 'the light of the world' (5:14)—presumably as reflectors of his light. At the death of Jesus, the whole scene was shrouded in darkness (Matthew 27:45) but, at his resurrection, the angel messenger shone 'like lightning' (Matthew 28:3). For the apostle Paul, the gospel of Christ is a 'light' and the hearts of believers are lit up by 'the light of the knowledge of the glory of God in the face of Jesus Christ' (2 Corinthians 4:4, 6).

In our passage today, Jesus is a 'light for revelation'. The word translated as 'revelation' is actually 'apocalypse'—an unfolding of a hidden truth. In Jesus, truth that was previously hidden from human understanding was made known—presumably the truth about the nature of God, which could only be revealed in human form. Jesus is what God is 'like', as we have already seen. In that child in the temple, less than six weeks old, the creator-God was pleased to reveal a whole new understanding of divinity.

Reflection

Revelation and glory were what Simeon's old eyes saw in the child in Mary's arms. May the eyes of faith today see in him unfolding truth and endless glory.

DW

Authority to forgive

'Why does this fellow speak in this way? It is blasphemy! Who can forgive sins but God alone?' At once Jesus perceived in his spirit that they were discussing these questions among themselves; and he said to them, '... Which is easier, to say to the paralytic, "Your sins are forgiven," or to say, "Stand up and take your mat and walk"? But so that you may know that the Son of Man has authority on earth to forgive sins'—he said to the paralytic—'I say to you, stand up, take your mat and go to your home.'

This is part of the story of one of Jesus' first miracles, the healing of a paralysed man. The questions are raised by a group of scribes who were present to give this new prophet a doctrinal check-up. Apparently Jesus failed at the first hurdle. Who did he think he was, forgiving sins? Surely only God could do that?

Their argument was partly true, partly false. Priests in the temple pronounced the forgiveness of sins and on the Day of Atonement the high priest declared all the sins of the people forgiven. It's true, however, that they did it in the name of God, rather than on their own authority. Jesus seemed to take that authority on himself, saying to the paralysed man, 'Your sins are forgiven'.

Jesus 'perceived in his spirit' what the scribes were saying. Far from denying the charge, he gladly accepted it. Only God can forgive and he was forgiving this man his sins, as a first step to healing his other, less pressing, handicap. He did it 'so that you may know that the Son of Man has authority on earth to forgive sins'.

Only God can heal a paralysed man; only God can forgive sins. If he—the 'Son of Man', a title Jesus used constantly to describe himself—could do the one, then he could do the other. So he said 'take up your mat and walk' and just as the visible paralysis was cured, his invisible sins were also healed. Only God could do the one; only God could do the other. They must draw their own conclusions!

Reflection

Who is Jesus? He is the Son of man (the true human, the image of the invisible God) who has power to forgive sins, thank God!

DW

Matthew 7:24, 28–29 (NRSV)

The teacher

'Everyone then who hears these words of mine and acts on them will be like a wise man who built his house on rock.'… Now when Jesus had finished saying these things, the crowds were astounded at his teaching, for he taught them as one having authority, and not as their scribes.

The one thing just about everyone agrees on is that Jesus was a great 'teacher'. Even those who belong to other faiths, or have no faith, will recognize that there is a sublime element to his ethical and moral teaching. In fact, it is unhelpful to disconnect the moral teaching of Jesus from everything else that he said and did. His call for moral perfection in the Sermon on the Mount (Matthew 5:48) would be simply demoralizing detached from his authority to forgive sin and his death on the cross—'Christ Jesus came into the world to save sinners' (1 Timothy 1:15).

That doesn't detract from the power and challenge of Jesus the Teacher, however. Although he performed miracles of healing, it seems to have been the authority of his teaching that most impressed the crowds. Each section of Matthew's Gospel that sets out those teachings ends with a similar kind of accolade: 'the crowds were astounded at his teaching'. The reason seems at first sight to be a strange one—'because he spoke with authority,

and not like the scribes'.

For the scribes, as indeed for Christian preachers, the authority was God's, not theirs. Their task was to interpret the sacred text and the Law and apply it to people's lives. Sadly, they fell for a temptation not unknown to preachers since then, which was to add to or complicate the Law so as to magnify their own office. Jesus, however, spoke on his own authority. 'You have heard that it was said…. But I say to you' (see Matthew 5:21, 27, 31, 38). By whom was it 'said'? By the Law, yet here was one who on his own authority reinterpreted that Law—an authority that truly lay with God alone. No wonder the people were 'astounded'.

Reflection

If Jesus did not speak with the authority of God, then his words are clearly blasphemous. If he did, though, then clearly he carried an authority greater than any human one. Were they truly listening to the voice of God?

DW

The healer

Now Simon's mother-in-law was in bed with a fever, and they told him [Jesus] about her at once. He came and took her by the hand and lifted her up. Then the fever left her, and she began to serve them. That evening, at sunset, they brought to him all who were sick or possessed with demons. And the whole city was gathered around the door. And he cured many who were sick with various diseases, and cast out many demons; and he would not permit the demons to speak, because they knew him.

Mark's opening chapter, at a breathless pace, introduces the ministry of Jesus in Galilee after his baptism. In the course of a single day, he exorcized a man in the synagogue, taught the crowds with such 'authority' that they were amazed, healed Simon Peter's mother-in-law of a fever and then conducted what seems to have been a mass healing outside Peter's house. Of course it was not, in the strict sense, 'mass' because each individual was dealt with according to his or her need, yet none was turned away and 'many' were cured. The next day, a leper came seeking cleansing and he was healed by the touch of Jesus—an action shunned by everyone else for fear of contamination (1:40–42).

That Jesus was known as a powerful 'healer' is a matter of historical record—Josephus, the historian of the Jews, mentions it. The biblical record is clear, however, in making a number of distinctions about this ministry. For instance, the Gospel writers say of some people to whom Jesus ministered that they had been 'cured' and of others that they were 'healed' or 'made whole'. These verbs translate different words in the original text. Those who were 'cured' found that their symptoms had gone—they were 'back to normal'. Those who were 'healed', on the other hand—often those who had shown great faith or gratitude, like the woman with the haemorrhage or the leper who stopped to give thanks—went away 'made whole' or 'saved', literally, because the two words share the same root. Jesus came to make people whole and that is much more (though not less) than curing their illnesses or ailments alone.

Sunday prayer

May the power of Jesus make me whole in body, mind and spirit.

DW

The Messiah

Jesus went on with his disciples to the villages of Caesarea Philippi; and on the way he asked his disciples, 'Who do people say that I am?' And they answered him, 'John the Baptist; and others, Elijah; and still others, one of the prophets.' He asked them, 'But who do you say that I am?' Peter answered him, 'You are the Messiah.' And he sternly ordered them not to tell anyone about him. Then he began to teach them that the Son of Man must undergo great suffering, and be rejected by the elders, the chief priests, and the scribes, and be killed, and after three days rise again.

'Who is Jesus?' we are asking in these readings. Here is the simplest answer, from the lips of Peter and in answer to a direct question by Jesus: 'You are the Messiah.' Matthew and Luke both add a little to the answer. In Matthew, Peter says, 'You are the Messiah, the Son of the living God' (16:16). In Luke the words are, 'The Messiah of God' (9:20). In all three cases, the answer amounts to the same, in essence: Jesus is the long-promised Saviour of Israel and the one God has sent to bring in a new kingdom of justice and righteousness.

We may find it hard to imagine the shocking nature of this revelation to the twelve disciples. These godly and orthodox Jewish men had been taught from their mother's laps that the God of Abraham would one day send a special delegate to restore the kingdom to Israel, a man endued with awesome authority and power.

Now they were walking along a country road with him! The man who was their friend was also the great prophet, the Messiah of God! Like most of them, he came from a poor background. Like them he had had little formal education, had no rank or title. Yet, almost instinctively, they seemed to know that he was different, special, marked with a quality that was more than merely human. There, on the dusty road to Caesarea Philippi, their unelected leader, Peter, put it into words: 'You are the Messiah.'

Reflection

What the disciples didn't know then, but were to learn later, was that the kingdom of God brought in by Jesus would be for all people, everywhere.

Their Messiah is also ours!

DW

45

The leader

They [the disciples] were on the road, going up to Jerusalem, and Jesus was walking ahead of them; they were amazed, and those who followed were afraid. He took the twelve aside again and began to tell them what was to happen to him, saying, 'See, we are going up to Jerusalem, and the Son of Man will be handed over to the chief priests and the scribes, and they will condemn him to death; then they will hand him over to the Gentiles; they will mock him, and spit upon him, and flog him, and kill him; and after three days he will rise again.'

The first call of Jesus to his disciples was crystal clear: 'Follow me!'—and they did, abandoning all for the sake of following the prophet from Galilee. At that time, they were full of hope. Here was the kind of leader who they, and all Israel, had been hoping for. He also had the endorsement of the immensely respected John the Baptist. Who knows what triumphs of faith and hope lay ahead?

At the point reached by today's reading, those optimistic ideas may have been somewhat amended. Just a few days before they had told him that they believed he was the Messiah. Surely now he would use some of the miraculous power they had seen employed to help the sick, the lame and the poor, to seize power from the Romans and their quisling supporters, the Herodian party? The people had waited so long—must they go on waiting and suffering for ever?

Then he broke it to them. Yes, he was the Messiah, but not the kind they had expected. He would not be a conquering king, in the style of David, but God's 'suffering servant', in line with the prophecies of Isaiah (53:4–9). His victory would be by sacrifice, not conquest. To achieve this, he was going to Jerusalem, even though opposition, suffering and death awaited him there.

At this point we might have excused the disciples if they had decided to look for another leader. Yet there was something about this one, in his dogged determination to do God's will whatever the cost, which made them hang on. Where he led, they would follow.

Reflection

'Lord, to whom can we go?' Peter asked, on another occasion. 'You have the words of eternal life' (John 6:68).

DW

Son of David

The crowds that went ahead of him [Jesus] and that followed were shouting, 'Hosanna to the Son of David! Blessed is the one who comes in the name of the Lord! Hosanna in the highest heaven!'… Then he [Jesus] said… 'How can they say that the Messiah is David's son? For David himself says in the book of Psalms, "The Lord said to my Lord, 'Sit at my right hand, until I make your enemies your footstool.'" David thus calls him Lord; so how can he be his son?'

We have already seen how Jesus called himself 'Son of man'—a title found in Daniel (7:13–14, NIV) to describe a human being given 'everlasting dominion' and 'a kingdom… that will never be destroyed'. Not surprisingly, the title was given messianic overtones. Here we find the crowds addressing Jesus as 'Son of David', expressing their longing for the restoration of an indestructible kingship exceeding in glory that of Israel's greatest king. To the annoyance of the watching teachers of the Law, Jesus didn't rebuke them. Indeed, he said that if the crowd were silenced in their cries, even 'the stones would shout out' (Luke 19:40).

Of course in one sense, by family line, Jesus was a descendant of David, but the crowds and the critics were both aware that in this context the phrase meant more. In the second passage above we find Jesus arguing that the Messiah is in fact more even than simply a 'Son of David'. The passage that he quotes had always been seen as speaking of the coming messiah, but understood in terms of restoring the kingdom of David. After 300 years of foreign conquest, such a restoration would be hugely popular with the people.

Jesus invites them to look more closely at the passage from a 'psalm of David'. In this, the great king speaks of 'the Lord' (God Almighty) but also of 'my Lord', who is invited to sit at God's right hand, in the place of honour, until all this person's enemies are made his 'footstool'. Obviously, Jesus argues, this second 'Lord' ('my Lord') is greater than David—so how can he be his 'son'? It would be hard to find clearer evidence of Jesus' claim that he is the Messiah.

Reflection

If this 'Son of David' is truly our king, then we owe him total loyalty and allegiance.

DW

47

The Lamb of God

The next day he [John the Baptist] saw Jesus coming towards him and declared, 'Here is the Lamb of God who takes away the sin of the world! This is he of whom I said, "After me comes a man who ranks ahead of me because he was before me." I myself did not know him; but I came baptizing with water for this reason, that he might be revealed to Israel.'

Perhaps this is the strangest answer to the question 'Who is Jesus?': 'the Lamb of God'. When we consider the qualities we normally look for in a leader, 'lamb-like' isn't one of them! We associate lambs with gambolling in fields, being weak and rather helpless. Lambs need care and nurture. Lions lead.

The first readers of John's Gospel wouldn't have interpreted the phrase in that way. For them, lambs were animals you sacrificed (or ate). The lamb made a good sacrificial offering because it was considered pure and unblemished, well qualified to bear the sins of others. Day by day in the temple in Jerusalem, 1000 priests offered an endless procession of such offerings—bulls and oxen (for their strength and financial value) and lambs for their purity. All day long the blood flowed and the smoke of the burnt offerings formed a constant pall over the building.

Jesus is the 'Lamb of God'. This speaks both of his utter purity of character and of his role as a sacrifice for our sins. Modern Christianity has tended to downplay this element in the Gospel—the very notion of sacrifices and blood being shed offending our sensitivities—but, if we do this, we then miss a vital element in the story of God's dealings with us. Jesus is the Lamb, but the Lamb 'of God'—God's gift of a lamb for the sacrifice. This may make us think of the story of Abraham and the possible sacrifice of his son Isaac: 'God himself will provide the lamb for a burnt-offering', the anxious boy was told—and, at the last possible minute, he did (Genesis 22:8, 13)!

Now, though, God was providing the perfect sacrifice for all our sins—his own sinless Son, who in eternity will share the throne of heaven with his Father as the lamb (Revelation 22:3).

Reflection

Lamb of God, you take away the sin of the world, have mercy on us.

DW

The suffering servant

Now the passage of the scripture that he was reading was this: 'Like a sheep he was led to the slaughter, and like a lamb silent before its shearer, so he does not open his mouth. In his humiliation justice was denied him. Who can describe his generation? For his life is taken away from the earth.' The eunuch asked Philip, 'About whom, may I ask you, does the prophet say this, about himself or about someone else?' Then Philip began to speak, and starting with this scripture, he proclaimed to him the good news about Jesus.

This reading follows on, in some ways, from yesterday's passage. The reader (in his chariot, on his way home from a visit to Jerusalem) is an Ethiopian eunuch. Presumably during his visit this Gentile seeker had acquired a scroll of the book of Isaiah and now, impatient to find what good things it contained, couldn't wait to read it. When Philip, prompted by God, approached him on the wayside, the eunuch was reading Isaiah 53 and had a crucial question to ask. About whom does the prophet say that he would be led like a lamb to the slaughter?

If Philip, a gifted evangelist, had been free to choose a single passage from the Hebrew scriptures on which to preach the good news about Jesus, it would have been this one. Not surprisingly, he leapt at the opportunity. By the time he had finished, the traveller was convinced. Philip baptized him by the roadside and the eunuch 'went on his way rejoicing' (v. 39). Many people believe that his conversion was at least partly responsible for the strong presence of Christianity in Ethiopia in the early centuries of the Church—which is still so today.

This passage shows how quickly the apostolic Church understood that Jesus did not come to be a conquering king type of a messiah, but what we might call 'the other model'. This is the 'Servant King' of Graham Kendrick's hymn, the one God sent 'not to be served, but to serve, and give [his] life that we might live'.

Reflection

Who is Jesus? Without doubt, the first Christians recognized that he was the Messiah of God, but it took them quite a long while to appreciate that his understanding of that role involved suffering and sacrifice rather than power and conquest.

DW

The name above every name

Therefore God also highly exalted him and gave him the name that is above every name, so that at the name of Jesus every knee should bend, in heaven and on earth and under the earth, and every tongue should confess that Jesus Christ is Lord, to the glory of God the Father.

Who is Jesus? We have found many answers, because there is no single one that could adequately describe him. Messiah, certainly; Son of God; our teacher; the one and only sacrifice for the sins of the world; and now, in this last reading, the one who is 'Lord'. Strangely, the word this is translated from can sometimes mean little more than 'Sir' or 'Master', yet, in this passage, as the culmination of a dramatic build-up of acclaim, it is evidently the highest honour that God could bestow.

These words follow the beautiful hymn on the humility of Christ, the one who 'emptied himself', who 'took the form of a slave' and became 'obedient to the point of death—even death on a cross' (vv. 7–8). The word 'therefore' links the two passages. As Jesus was obedient to the will of the Father, because he was prepared to die a cruel and humiliating death as a criminal, *therefore* God 'also highly exalted him'. He ranked the name 'Jesus'—Saviour—'above every name', a name at which one day every knee will bow and every tongue confess that he is 'Lord'. All of this will be 'to the glory of God the Father'.

In this way, the full title of Jesus is set down for us: Lord Jesus Christ. He is Jesus, the Saviour—the name given by the angel to Mary and Joseph. He is Christ, the Messiah sent by God to bring in the new kingdom of justice and peace. He is also Lord, one whom we worship as divine. He earned the honour on the cross, but it is the risen and ascended Lord Jesus who now sits 'on the right hand of the Majesty on high' (Hebrews 1:3).

Reflection

Even unbelievers and sceptics concede that Jesus was a holy man, a great teacher and a splendid example to follow, yet this good and holy man also truly believed that he was the Messiah and the Son of God and Christians believe him, too, which is why we worship and follow him.

DW

Song of Songs: deeper into love

I have a confession to make. I enjoy a good love story! In fact, my favourite film is *You've Got Mail*—a romantic comedy starring Tom Hanks and Meg Ryan. Perhaps that is why I have been asked to contribute these notes on the Song of Songs!

It seems that King Solomon, too, was a romantic at heart. He wrote over 1000 songs (1 Kings 4:32), but this love song is the most enduring. It is, however, an unusual piece to be included in the Bible. It doesn't mention God and is never quoted elsewhere in scripture. It contains no teaching or doctrine and there is little in terms of a storyline to grab our attention. Why, then, is it here and why has it been a favourite with many great devotional writers?

First, it reminds us of the sanctity of human love. It affirms that sex is good, human relationships are important and God takes pleasure in the fact that he made us 'male and female' (Genesis 1:27). Read like this, it helps us to celebrate the union of two people in marriage, shows that Christian teaching about sex is overwhelmingly positive and provides an alternative to the loveless sex of a permissive society.

Second, at a deeper level, it gives us a wonderful picture of the love between God and Israel (Isaiah 54:5–6: 'your Maker is your husband'); Christ and the Church (Ephesians 5:23–25: 'Husbands, love your wives, just as Christ loved the church and gave himself up for her'); and Jesus and the individual believer (Galatians 2:20: 'the Son of God, who loved me and gave himself for me'). We will follow this third line of interpretation and hear in the words of the song a call to intimacy with our Saviour.

It is notoriously difficult to analyse this text. Some see three main characters (the Shulamite maiden, her lover the shepherd and a rival who is Solomon), while others identify just two people (the maiden and her lover, King Solomon). We will be using the NIV translation, which adopts the second position.

Love is at the heart of the Christian life. It begins with the discovery of God's love for us personally, grows into our responsive love for him and then issues in an outflow of love to those around us. As you read, may you find your passion for Jesus being reignited.

Tony Horsfall

Hungry for love

Beloved: Let him kiss me with the kisses of his mouth—for your love is more delightful than wine. Pleasing is the fragrance of your perfumes; your name is like perfume poured out. No wonder the maidens love you! Take me away with you—let us hurry! Let the king bring me into his chambers.

We are introduced at the beginning of the song to the girl in question—called the 'Beloved' by the NIV translators because she is the object of the king's affection. We know little about her apart from the fact that she is an ordinary girl from Shulem ('Shulammite', 6:13), growing up in an ordinary family in a rural setting (1:6). What is clear from the start is that she is passionately in love with Solomon, and he with her. Here she fantasizes about him, impatient to be with him and to receive tangible expressions (kisses) of his love. She is acutely lovesick.

Wanting to be loved is a basic human need. We all cry out for intimacy, to know that we have worth and value in the eyes of someone else. Romantic love seems to offer to meet that need and most of us assume that if we were happily married, the aching inside us for love would be instantly met. It is true, of course, that human relationships go a long way towards meeting that need, but ultimately no other person can love us perfectly. For our need to be fully satisfied, we have to look to the one who is the lover of our souls.

The yearning of the girl for her lover is a picture to us, therefore, of our greater need to discover intimacy with God through Jesus Christ. It is possible to know that we are loved by God as he declares this to be the case (see Romans 5:8, for example). It is also wonderfully possible to experience that love personally through the work of the Holy Spirit (Romans 5:5). We can both know it in our head and feel it in our hearts. The challenge of the Song of Songs is to combine facts with feelings, so that mind and emotions can both bear witness to the love of God.

Sunday prayer

As I ponder these words, Lord, reveal to me afresh the reality of your unceasing love towards me.

TH

SONG OF SONGS 1:5–6 (NIV)

Does he really love me?

Beloved: Dark am I, yet lovely, O daughters of Jerusalem, dark like the tents of Kedar, like the tent curtains of Solomon. Do not stare at me because I am dark, because I am darkened by the sun. My mother's sons were angry with me and made me take care of the vineyards; my own vineyard I have neglected.

We sense here a moment of hesitancy, of self-doubt in the maiden, which most of us can identify with. We ask ourselves, 'How attractive am I?' and wonder 'Am I really worth loving?' She knows of her love for the king, but could he possibly love her in return? It seems too good to be true.

What troubles her most is her swarthy appearance. She has worked long hours in the vineyard and is self-consciously aware that she is now very tanned and, she imagines, less attractive. True love, however, looks beyond externals. Some commentators take the words 'yet lovely' to be an interjection by Solomon. It seems that he is not at all put off by what he sees. Rather, his love accepts her as she is.

One of the key moments in the journey towards intimacy is the realization that we are accepted as we are. Although it is a vulnerable place to be, we can only know we are loved when we openly acknowledge our weaknesses, shortcomings and failures before the one we love.

The love of God is totally unconditional. He knows everything about us and loves us just the same. In the presence of Jesus, we can come clean about our sin and wrongdoing and yet still be completely accepted. We can allow our darkness to surface in the knowledge that nothing we have done will make him love us any less. We meet only forgiveness, cleansing, understanding and mercy. Guilt and shame melt away in this healing grace.

We may feel unworthy of his love and undeserving. Past mistakes may seem to haunt us and disqualify us. Sometimes the hardest thing is to allow ourselves to be loved and, as someone has said, to 'accept our acceptance'. This is the first step on the road to intimacy. Do not be afraid to trust that you are loved.

Prayer

Father, help me to understand that your love for me really is unconditional—no strings attached.

TH

Words of love

Lover: How beautiful you are, my darling! Oh, how beautiful! Your eyes are doves.
Beloved: How handsome you are, my lover! Oh how charming! And our bed is verdant.
Lover: The beams of our house are cedars; our rafters are firs.
Beloved: I am a rose of Sharon, a lily of the valleys.
Lover: Like a lily among thorns is my darling among the maidens.

Today is Valentine's Day. All over the world, cards will be arriving that speak of love. Some will be sent for fun, some out of duty and many out of hope! Even if sent anonymously, most will have been chosen for the beauty and appropriateness of the words.

Words are not everything when it comes to expressing love, but they are important and this little dialogue is a passionate exchange between the king (Lover) and the maiden (Beloved). Each of us has our own particular 'love language' that we like to use to give and receive love. This may include physical touch, acts of kindness, the giving of presents, spending time together and so on. Few of us mind being told how much we are loved, though, and we cannot hear such affirmation too often. When it comes to love, most of us need lots of verbal reassurances.

If you can place yourself in the position of the Shulammite girl, perhaps you can receive these words as spoken to you by your heavenly king, Jesus, the true lover of your soul. He has many ways of communicating his love, but he speaks tenderly and repeatedly through scripture to affirm his passionate affection for us. Take time to listen to what he is saying to you and recognize that you are his beloved.

If you can make that step, perhaps you can go further and use the Beloved's words to speak back your love to the Saviour, for he loves to receive our worship and adoration. We love because he first loved us (1 John 4:19). As we recognize his grace towards us (his 'charm'), so we begin to appreciate how worthy he is of our praise.

Why not start a dialogue of love with Jesus? This is the heart of prayer and the beginning of spiritual intimacy.

Prayer
Lord, I receive your love and in return give you my heartfelt praise.

TH

Love's resting place

Beloved: Like an apple tree among the trees of the forest is my lover among the young men. I delight to sit in his shade, and his fruit is sweet to my taste. He has taken me to the banquet hall, and his banner over me is love. Strengthen me with raisins, refresh me with apples, for I am faint with love. His left arm is under my head, and his right arm embraces me.

As their relationship deepens, the maiden's wish now becomes reality—she is brought into the king's chambers, to his banqueting hall. A lavish display of kindness and generosity assures her of his love. It is as if the canopy stretched over them is embroidered with the words 'I love you'.

This assurance allows the maiden to relax in the king's presence. They embrace and she leans on him, content in his love and safe in his arms. It is a moment of pure bliss, one of which she has dreamt, and she does not want it to be disturbed (v. 7).

In the growing relationship between the believer and the Lord, there are also moments of deep intimacy, of assurance of being loved. Once we have learned to take God at his word, to believe that he really does love us, we find we can begin to relax in his presence and our souls find rest. We are no longer striving to please him or straining to earn his favour, but discovering that we can lean on him, like the beloved disciple (John 21:20). We bask in his acceptance, delight in his forgiveness and rest in his unchanging love.

This is what it means to abide in Christ and in his love (John 15:9). It is what the apostle John meant when he spoke of being 'perfected' in love (1 John 4:18)—that happy state of knowing that we are safe and secure because we have been loved unconditionally and eternally. Having found such a place, we do not easily want to surrender it.

Take a moment now to relax yourself in the presence of the one who loves you so well. Rest in this place of loving acceptance. See yourself, however unworthy, as the object of divine love.

Prayer

Lord, I linger in your presence, and rest in your embrace.

TH

Invitation to intimacy

Beloved: Listen! My lover! Look! Here he comes, leaping across the mountains, bounding over the hills. My lover is like a gazelle or a young stag. Look! There he stands behind our wall, gazing through the windows, peering through the lattice. My lover spoke and said to me, 'Arise, my darling, my beautiful one, and come with me. See! The winter is past; the rains are over and gone. Flowers appear on the earth; the season of singing has come….'

Everyone knows that it takes time and effort for a relationship to develop. Two people can only become close if they spend time together and make their relationship a priority. This requires letting go of lesser priorities.

For the first time in the song we are given an insight into the king's passion for the maiden. He comes bounding across the hills to invite her to be with him. It is springtime (vv. 11–13) and he longs to be with his chosen one, to spend time enjoying her company. Love is in the air and he longs for her presence.

It may seem strange to some to realize that God longs to have fellowship with us, that he is passionate about meeting with us, but it is true. He made us to have fellowship with himself. The essence of eternal life is that we 'know' both Father and Son in a deeply personal way (John 17:3). We should not be surprised, then, if we find the Holy Spirit gently calling us to spend time alone with God, inviting us into intimacy with our Saviour.

Many people these days have a growing desire to take time out to concentrate on their inner life, to learn to be still and focus more on God (Psalm 46:10). They are discovering the value of quiet days and retreats, slowing down a little and seeking a more balanced approach to life. Some, so busy serving God that they have neglected to be with him, are making radical adjustments to their lifestyles. They realize that making space for God is vital for greater spiritual intimacy and high on the Holy Spirit's agenda for the contemporary Church.

If you hear that gentle voice drawing you aside, do not hesitate to respond.

Prayer

Lord, save me from the danger of being too busy for you.

TH

SONG OF SONGS 2:16–17 (NIV)

Ready to commit

Beloved: My lover is mine and I am his; he browses among the lilies. Until the day breaks and the shadows flee, turn, my lover, and be like a gazelle or like a young stag on the rugged hills.

With these words we seem to reach a very special moment in the relationship between the two lovers—a moment of commitment, perhaps even of betrothal. 'My lover is mine and I am his' seems to indicate that they are now ready for the surrender that love invites. Soon we will hear of the wedding day (3:11) and the maiden will become the bride (4:8). Here is the progression of love.

It is easy to forget how frightening the idea of commitment is to some people. For those who have only known broken relationships, the idea of giving oneself exclusively to another is very disconcerting. This is why many shy away from marriage, preferring casual relationships. Even in long-term relationships, there may be a fear of the commitment that marriage requires. For love to reach its full maturity, however, there must be a willing surrender by both parties.

As we follow the relationship between the maiden and the king further, we will notice the maturing of their love—especially when viewed through the eyes of the girl.

True love cannot be stationary; it must either grow or decline.

In the statement 'My lover is mine and I am his', we see the first stage of love. This is love received and the focus is on self—what the other person gives to me. Later, the girl will say 'I am my lover's and my lover is mine' (6:3), the order being reversed, and there being a second stage where love is both given and received. Eventually, she declares simply, 'I belong to my lover' (7:10)—an indication of her abandonment to her husband in self-giving love, which is the third and deepest stage in a relationship.

It has been said that this ability to care deeply for others and place their interests ahead of our own is the highpoint of personal maturity and psychological development. In our relationship with God, it is the goal of our discipleship and the evidence of our union with Christ.

Prayer

Lord, take away my fear of commitment. Let me joyfully give myself to you and others.

TH

Losing touch

Beloved: All night long on my bed I looked for the one my heart loves; I looked for him but did not find him. I will get up now and go about the city, through its streets and squares; I will search for the one my heart loves. So I looked for him but did not find him. The watchmen found me as they made their rounds in the city. 'Have you seen the one my heart loves?' Scarcely had I passed them when I found the one my heart loves. I held him and would not let him go till I had brought him to my mother's house, to the room of the one who conceived me.

There is no doubting the maiden's love for her betrothed, judging by the oft-repeated phrase 'the one my heart loves', but here she seems to have fallen into the trap of taking his love for granted. Perhaps life in the city had provided some distractions for her. Perhaps she had become complacent, even a little lazy ('I will get up now', v. 2). Whatever the reason, she is out of touch with her lover.

It is easy to become disconnected from the place of intimacy with Jesus. Many things crowd into our lives—all demanding our attention in different ways. Material possessions steal our hearts, exciting pastimes divert our energies. It is not that we lose our love for God, but more that it may become lukewarm (Revelation 3:15–16). Strangely, the knowledge that God loves us unconditionally can cause us to take his love for granted, too. Our attitude can all too easily end up as, 'If God loves me anyway, why bother to seek him earnestly?'

Spiritual growth requires effort on our part. The exercise of spiritual disciplines—prayer, Bible reading, fellowship with other Christians, service, silence, solitude and so on—place us in the position where God's love and grace can continue to flow towards us. They help us create a climate for intimacy.

If you have somehow lost touch with the Saviour, do not worry. As soon as you seek him, you will find him (Jeremiah 29:13; Isaiah 55:6). When you find him again, hold on to him this time.

Prayer

Forgive my complacency, Lord. Set my heart to seek you fully.

TH

SONG OF SONGS 3:6–11 (NIV)

The bridegroom arrives

Beloved: Who is this coming up from the desert like a column of smoke, perfumed with myrrh and incense made from all the spices of the merchant? Look! It is Solomon's carriage, escorted by 60 warriors, the noblest of Israel, all of them wearing the sword, all experienced in battle… King Solomon made for himself the carriage; he made it of wood from Lebanon. Its posts he made of silver, its base of gold… Come out, you daughters of Zion, and look at King Solomon wearing the crown, the crown with which his mother crowned him on the day of his wedding, the day his heart rejoiced.

With fitting splendour, King Solomon arrives for his wedding day, escorted by his elite bodyguard. This is a royal wedding and the grandeur of the occasion reminds us that he is the king. 'Solomon is coming, carried on his throne' (v. 7, GNB). Power and wealth are his and no expense is spared in the display of his glory. This is a most happy moment, too, for his heart rejoices as he meets his bride.

Onlookers are invited to observe the occasion, come out and gaze on the wonderful scene, be impressed by his majesty. How the bride must have delighted in what she saw! Here is a husband to be proud of, one who can protect her and provide for her, one to whom she can confidently give herself, one on whom she can safely depend.

Contemplation has been defined as 'the prayer of loving attentiveness'. It provides us with the opportunity to gaze on the Saviour and remind ourselves of his position as the king enthroned in heaven. He is the one who wears the crown. As we turn our eyes on Jesus, we remind ourselves of his power to protect us and his ability to meet our every need. When we fix our gaze on him, our love for him is increased and we are strengthened enough to persevere.

Take time today to gaze afresh on the exalted Lord Jesus. Remind yourself that he is worthy of your praise and trust. He is the one who reigns on high, with everything beneath his control. Worship his majesty!

Sunday prayer

Let me see you as you are, Lord, risen and exalted.

TH

SONG OF SONGS 4:1, 7, 9–10 (NIV)

Portrait of the bride

Lover: How beautiful you are, my darling! Oh, how beautiful! Your eyes behind your veil are doves. Your hair is like a flock of goats descending from Mount Gilead…. All beautiful you are, my darling; there is no flaw in you…. You have stolen my heart, my sister, my bride; you have stolen my heart with one glance of your eyes, with one jewel of your necklace. How delightful is your love, my sister, my bride!

A wise retreat leader posed this question: 'What do you think God feels about you?' Some participants replied with words such as 'disappointed', 'frustrated' and even 'angry'.

'The truth is,' he said, 'when God thinks of you, love swells in his heart and a smile comes to his face.'

We see in these verses the absolute delight the bridegroom takes in his bride—a reminder to us of the delight that God takes in us. Is this description overdone? Is it true that there is no flaw in her or is it simply that love is blind?

If we are to grow in intimacy with God, we must learn to see ourselves as he sees us. How *does* God see us? He sees us as we are 'in Christ'—that is, our lives made one with his and his righteousness imparted to us. This is our true identity. At conversion, God took away our unrighteousness and gave us the gift of his own right-eousness: 'God made him who

had no sin to be sin for us, so that in him we might become the right-eousness of God' (2 Corinthians 5:21; also Romans 5:19; Philippians 3:9; Colossians 1:22).

It is not our behaviour (sinful or otherwise) that first catches God's attention, but our identity as his beloved ones—those who have been made righteous by their inclusion in Christ. It is this knowledge that gives us the confidence to come before him in worship and prayer, serve him with gladness and become more fully the people he has made us to be. This is the 'beauty' of the bride.

Learn to recognize yourself as one who is amazingly loved by God and has received, by grace, the gift of righteousness. It is who you really are! (See 1 John 3:1.)

Prayer

Thank you, Lord, that you take delight in me and love me passionately.

TH

SONG OF SONGS 4:12—5:1 (NIV)

The fruits of love

Lover: You are a garden locked up, my sister, my bride; you are a spring enclosed, a sealed fountain. Your plants are an orchard of pomegranates with choice fruits, with henna and nard, nard and saffron, calamus and cinnamon, with every kind of incense tree, with myrrh and aloes and all the finest spices. You are a garden fountain, a well of flowing water streaming down from Lebanon.
Beloved: Awake, north wind, and come, south wind! Blow on my garden, that its fragrance may spread abroad. Let my lover come into his garden and taste its choice fruits.
Lover: I have come into my garden, my sister, my bride: I have gathered my myrrh with my spice....

By means of the metaphor of the garden (perhaps an echo of Eden?) we are introduced to the satisfaction that committed love can bring.

The tender care bestowed on his wife by the loving husband causes her to grow and blossom as a person. It is a life-giving relationship, releasing her into her full potential (the fruits and spices). For her part, she is happy to give her affection exclusively to her husband (a garden locked) and, indeed, desires that the winds blow on her, releasing the fragrance of her love towards him. Each finds joy and delight in self-giving love towards the other.

We find our own true fulfilment as individuals when we surrender ourselves fully to the love of God. His only desire is to restore his image within us and make our lives fruitful. This he does through the Holy Spirit, who begins to form the life of Christ within us. The beautiful list of the fruits of the Spirit (Galatians 5:22–23) is really a description of the life of Christ.

Should the cold north wind of adversity blows on us, we can release the fragrance of our love for him by remaining steadfast, trusting in his goodness no matter what our circumstances. Likewise, when the warm, balmy winds of blessing caress our lives, the praise and worship of our grateful hearts is a delight to him. Our choice to bless the Lord at all times (Psalm 34:1) gives great satisfaction to the lover of our souls.

Prayer

Rain or shine, I choose to bless your name, O Lord. Take delight in me, I pray.

TH

The lover disappears

Beloved: I slept but my heart was awake. Listen! My lover is knocking: 'Open to me, my sister, my darling, my dove, my flawless one. My head is drenched with dew, my hair with the dampness of the night.' I have taken off my robe—must I put it on again? I have washed my feet—must I soil them again? My lover thrust his hand through the latch-opening; my heart began to pound for him. I arose to open for my lover... my fingers... on the handles of the lock... but my lover had left; he was gone. My heart sank at his departure. I looked for him but did not find him. I called him but he did not answer.

The honeymoon is truly over now! After the ecstasy of shared love comes the painful realization that the path of true love does not always run smoothly. The unwillingness of the bride to put herself out for her husband causes her to miss the opportunity to respond to his invitation to share in what he is doing.

Those who have walked the path of intimacy with God before us often testify to moments of ecstasy when the presence of God is almost unbearable. They also speak of what some have called 'the dark night of the soul', when all emotional awareness of God is seemingly lost. For those who have known such intense closeness to God, this separation is extremely painful and baffling.

It seems that there are several things to learn from what is a perfectly normal experience. First, we must not depend on our emotions alone in our search for God. He is near, whether we feel him or not. Second, his 'felt' absence does not imply that he is angry with us—merely that he is purifying our faith and doing deeper work in our hearts. Third, the consciousness of his presence will eventually return and our love for him will be even deeper. Absence does make the heart grow fonder.

Of course, we do not choose to experience such moments of apparent abandonment but, if they come, we can understand them more and set our hearts to love God as much in his apparent absence as in his certain presence.

Prayer

In the darkness my soul reaches out to you, faithful God.

TH

My lover, my friend

Friends: How is your beloved better than others, most beautiful of women…?

Beloved: My lover is radiant and ruddy, outstanding among ten thousand. His head is purest gold; his hair is wavy and black as a raven. His eyes are like doves by the water streams, washed in milk, mounted like jewels. His cheeks are like beds of spice… His arms are rods of gold… His body is like polished ivory… His legs are pillars of marble… His mouth is sweetness itself; he is altogether lovely. This is my lover, this my friend, O daughters of Jerusalem.

Friends: Where has your lover gone, most beautiful of women…?

Beloved: My lover has gone down to his garden… I am my lover's and he is mine; he browses among the lilies.

The temporary absence of her husband has convinced the bride how much she really does love him and the poetic description she gives of him emphasizes in particular his stability and reliability. The experience has also moved her into a deeper place of love, where the emphasis is now on him rather than on her and she is ready to offer herself to him more completely than ever before. Her love is maturing.

Commentators sometimes make a great deal of the imagery used in this description of the lover, drawing all kinds of parallels with other scriptures that speak of the qualities of Jesus. Space does not allow us that luxury here, so we shall have to be content with getting the general impression that these verses convey—that of someone who is unique and outstanding, utterly faithful, reliable and worthy of the strongest affection. Jesus is all these things and much, much more.

We can see, too, that love and friendship go hand-in-hand. It is a wonderful testimony to be able to introduce others to Jesus by saying, 'This is my lover, this my friend.' It suggests a relationship that has been tried and tested and has come through the storms intact. It has been proven in the hard places of life and is therefore all the more attractive to others. He, and he alone, is the friend who loves at all times, the one who sticks closer than any other human being (Proverbs 17:17 and 18:24).

Prayer

Help me to commend you to others today, my lover and my friend.

TH

Oneness

Beloved: May the wine go straight to my lover, flowing gently over lips and teeth. I belong to my lover, and his desire is for me. Come, my lover, let us go to the countryside, let us spend the night in the villages. Let us go early to the vineyards to see if the vines have budded, if their blossoms have opened, and if the pomegranates are in bloom—there I will give you my love.

Friends: Who is this coming up from the desert leaning on her lover?

Maturity in love can be described as a shift in the focus from 'me' to an awareness of 'we'. The bride seems now to have reached this stage in that she can say confidently 'I belong to my lover', without any reference back to herself. She takes the initiative to be with him. They share together in the work of the vineyard. Their lives blend together and she speaks of 'us'. The two have become one in every way.

Union with God is the goal of the spiritual life, by which we mean a growing awareness of the fact that we have been joined to Christ and share his life (1 Corinthians 6:17). For this to be worked out, we must offer ourselves up to God as fully and freely as we are able. This surrender is a surrender to love and we need not be afraid that God will take advantage of us or abuse us in some way. We freely give him our love in the knowledge that he has already freely given his love to us.

This brings us to a place of rest and dependency, of leaning on our beloved. This posture is one that should characterize our relationship with Jesus. We are to lean heavily on his grace, depending on him to work in and through us to achieve all that he wants us to do, resting moment by moment in the assurance of his unchanging love.

In this context, we can be workers working together with God—not working for him, but with him. Far from leading us into passivity, intimacy with God moves us into action. We want to be where our lover is and share in what he is doing.

Prayer

Lord, today I lean the full weight of my life on you.

TH

SONG OF SONGS 8:6–7, 11–14 (NIV, ABRIDGED)

Mine to give

[*Beloved:*] Place me like a seal over your heart... for love is as strong as death, its jealousy unyielding as the grave. It burns like blazing fire, like a mighty flame. Many waters cannot quench love; rivers cannot wash it away.... Solomon had a vineyard in Baal Hamon; he let out his vineyard to tenants. Each was to bring for its fruit a thousand shekels of silver. But my own vineyard is mine to give.... Come away, my lover, and be like a gazelle or like a young stag on the spice-laden mountains.

As we come to the close of this wonderful book, with its beautiful poetry and symbolism, we see how the love between the maiden and Solomon has developed, from the romance of courtship, to the joy of wedded bliss and on to the self-sacrificing love of the mature couple. At each stage, we have seen similarities between this relationship and the believer's relationship with the Lord.

Here we are reminded that love is passionate. It burns with intensity, lasting through the severest of trials. Such love, burning in the hearts of God's people, has motivated them to perform the most heroic of deeds and endure the fiercest of persecutions, even to the point of martyrdom.

We are reminded, too, that love is generous. Wealthy Solomon has no need of money from his bride and, unlike the tenant farmers, she is under no obligation to share the income from her vineyard with him. She chooses to do so freely and joyfully. It is the gift of her love, offered willingly and without duress.

We know that God loves a cheerful giver (2 Corinthians 9:7). We are under no compulsion to give ourselves to him. Our money, time, abilities and possessions are, in a sense, given freely to us. We can cling tightfistedly to them or open-handedly offer them to God. If we give them back to him, we do so because we choose to, not because we have to. This is what makes the gift of our lives so special to God. They are ours to give. The fact that I chose to live for God, rather than for myself, is an indication that his love has truly won my heart.

Prayer

Lord, kindle a flame of sacred love within my heart. Let it burn there unceasingly for your glory.

TH

The signs of the times

I used to be a history teacher. To some of you that will mean I must know all about dates. Well, I need to confess that, at my university entrance interview, the interviewer looked at me slightly quizzically and said, 'There aren't many facts in your essays, but we're sure you know them!' I smiled quietly back. Who was I to argue?

Dates and facts are the stuff of history, but what makes some so significant? Most people have heard of 1066—the year of the Battle of Hastings and the victory of William the Conqueror—but on that misty morning in October, over 900 years ago, how many people realized that it would turn out to be a pivotal moment in the history of England?

That's one of the roles of the prophet—bringing divine insight to human activity, discerning the significant from the routine. The prophet spots the meaningful trend from the humdrum and repetitious, then highlights it on behalf of God, giving people the opportunity to respond.

Prophecy is not so much about predicting the future as offering the possibility of changing it by interpreting the present. It means seeing the world as God sees it. Joseph was given the understand-ing of a dream: he was in an Egyptian prison one moment and, the next, prime minister and saving the lives of thousands.

When you read the Old Testament, you discover that the prophetic task could be even more profound than this. Prophets were called to more than insight and speaking out. For some, it meant acting out a parable for a few days, weeks, even years. For Hosea, his whole life became a sign.

As far as many Christians today are concerned, prophecy is a hot potato. Do we still have prophets? If so, what weight should we give to their words? Over the next few days, we'll be exploring the theme of prophecy in the Bible. We'll see that God chose people to speak his words. What's more, he chose specific individuals to speak through their lives.

In that sense, we all have a prophetic role. God still calls people to live for him and, thus, become God's message to the world. The prophets of old would have understood the challenge of Francis of Assisi: 'Preach the gospel always; when necessary use words.' The Church should always be a sign for the times.

Stephen Rand

MATTHEW 16:1–4 (NIV)

Reading the signs

The Pharisees and Sadducees came to Jesus and tested him by asking him to show them a sign from heaven. He replied, 'When evening comes, you say, "It will be fair weather, for the sky is red," and in the morning, "Today it will be stormy, for the sky is red and overcast." You know how to interpret the appearance of the sky, but you cannot interpret the signs of the times. A wicked and adulterous generation looks for a miraculous sign, but none will be given it except the sign of Jonah.' Jesus then left them and went away.

So we are all prophets! Who has not looked up at a glowing sunset and pronounced sagely, 'Red sky at night, shepherd's delight'? I don't think, though, that I have ever thought that I was quoting Jesus and referring to a weather forecasting method going back at least 2000 years.

Jesus was contrasting the ease with which human beings claim to interpret climatic phenomenon with their difficulty at discerning the 'signs of the times', yet everything that he had been doing and saying during his earthly ministry was a sign. His words and works revealed the very nature of God—a signpost of the kingdom. In fact, not so much a signpost as a giant illuminated Piccadilly Circus-style announcement.

The problem was not the lack of a sign. The problem was people's unwillingness, their inability—or perhaps their deliberate refusal—to see the obvious.

In the desert, Jesus had been tempted by the devil to perform miracles. Now, the religious leaders were repeating the process. Both were looking for Jesus to opt for the shortcut. Perhaps both instinctively knew that, because his message was uncompromising but life-giving and world-changing, the best tactic was to sidetrack Jesus and substitute entertainment for reality.

The sign that they were offered was the sign of Jonah—the prophet who came back from the death that was the belly of a great fish and saw a multitude rescued from God's judgment. Resurrection was to be the greatest sign of all—a miraculous sign indeed, but not everyone would recognize it.

Sunday prayer

Resurrected Lord, help us to see the signs that you are at work—in our world, our churches, our lives. Help us to embrace your work, not resist it.

SR

The sign of Jonah

The word of the Lord came to Jonah son of Amittai: 'Go to the great city of Nineveh and preach against it, because its wickedness has come up before me.' But Jonah ran away from the Lord and headed for Tarshish… Then the Lord sent a great wind on the sea, and such a violent storm arose that the ship threatened to break up… So [the sailors] asked [Jonah], 'What should we do to you to make the sea calm down for us?' 'Pick me up and throw me into the sea', he replied, 'and it will become calm. I know that it is my fault that this great storm has come upon you.' … But the Lord provided a great fish to swallow Jonah, and Jonah was inside the fish three days and three nights.

Ask anyone what they know about Jonah and they will tell you about a whale—a creature that doesn't actually appear in the story! It's a great children's tale, one I love to use with them, but Jesus twice referred his accusers to the sign of Jonah (Matthew 12:39; 16:4), so it is worth adults taking his story seriously, too.

The first thing to note is that God was concerned about a distant city, outsiders, even enemies. This was—and is—a major teaching point. All too often, God's people think that they have been chosen because they are special, rather than chosen to be God's special people because they carry out his purposes in reaching out to others.

Second, Jonah turned his back on God, but God rescued him and gave him another chance. Many Christians are acutely aware of their failures, but the story of Jonah is a sign that God is in the forgiving and restoring business. The people of Nineveh learned that from Jonah and took their second chance, much to Jonah's disgust (see chapters 3 and 4).

Jonah is a sign to us that God is concerned about the great mass of people and that he's concerned about each individual. Jonah tells us that a prophet will share God's concerns, a prophet will know God's forgiveness and renewal for service and a prophet will speak out and live out the word of God. A prophet may even see God at work in a way that they never expected.

Reflection

How does God want Jonah to be a sign to you?

SR

Show us a sign

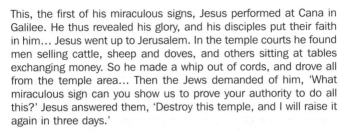

This, the first of his miraculous signs, Jesus performed at Cana in Galilee. He thus revealed his glory, and his disciples put their faith in him... Jesus went up to Jerusalem. In the temple courts he found men selling cattle, sheep and doves, and others sitting at tables exchanging money. So he made a whip out of cords, and drove all from the temple area... Then the Jews demanded of him, 'What miraculous sign can you show us to prove your authority to do all this?' Jesus answered them, 'Destroy this temple, and I will raise it again in three days.'

It was a simple equation: prophets did miracles, so a miracle proved that you were a prophet. In John's Gospel, the Greek word translated 'miracle' is also translated as 'sign', which all sounds very reasonable.

What seems less reasonable is Jesus' logic. In Cana, he turns water into wine. Then he goes to Jerusalem, creates a scene in the temple and refuses to produce a miracle when asked. Instead, he offers a statement that is enigmatic—and undoubtedly provocative.

What is going on? John is unequivocal. The memorable wedding celebration had 'revealed his glory', but scholars still debate quite how. You would have to be a very single-minded wine buff to believe that the creation of an instant vintage in itself revealed Jesus' glory. Perhaps the sheer quantity indicates his overflowing generosity; perhaps the endorsement of a family celebration is a sign of the fullness of life God wills for all creation.

In the family home, he shares his joy. In his Father's house, he reveals his anger. This is a different sign: a sign of God's values. When money replaces God at the heart of worship, then perhaps the miracle was his restraint rather than his anger.

The very act of cleansing the temple in fact revealed his authority: this was the son defending his Father's name. The demand for a sign revealed the people's unbelief. Their demands would lead to a cross, where again his glory would be revealed, even as his 'temple' was being destroyed. Then came the ultimate sign of his glory and authority: rising after three days.

Prayer

Father, forgive us when we demand evidence of your goodness and have failed to recognize the signs of blessing all around us. Amen

SR

The sign of the cross

But whatever was to my profit I now consider loss for the sake of Christ. What is more, I consider everything a loss compared to the surpassing greatness of knowing Christ Jesus my Lord, for whose sake I have lost all things. I consider them rubbish, that I may gain Christ and be found in him, not having a righteousness of my own that comes from the law, but that which is through faith in Christ— the righteousness that comes from God and is by faith. I want to know Christ and the power of his resurrection and the fellowship of sharing in his sufferings, becoming like him in his death, and so, somehow, to attain to the resurrection from the dead.

The apostle Paul had given up the advantages of his birth, education, citizenship. However, he had gained something he believed to be far more valuable—the presence of Jesus as his friend and Lord.

He recognized that this was the precise mirror image of what Jesus had done for him. Jesus had voluntarily given up all things— heaven for earth, life for death—so that it would be possible for Paul, and millions more like him, to receive everything—eternal life— as the experience and result of his life-giving friendship.

This is reflected in the sign of Ash Wednesday when the joyful expectation symbolized in the waving palm branches of Palm Sunday turned to the ashes of betrayal and abandonment in a matter of days. In the act of losing, however, Jesus was gaining everything. The ashes that symbolize death are also a sign of the repentance that makes it possible to receive the gift of eternal life—the power of the resurrection.

On Ash Wednesday, worshippers receive the sign of the cross on their foreheads. In some traditions it is then washed off as a sign of being cleansed from sin. In others, it is carried out into the world as a sign of identification with Christ in his death for all to see. Paul would have approved of both ways. He knew that, with his sins forgiven, he could be certain of the presence of Jesus.

Prayer

Lord Jesus, give us that longing for your presence and grant us greater understanding of what it means to share in your sufferings and carry the sign of your cross. Amen

SR

MICAH 6:2–8 (NRSV, ABRIDGED)

The prophetic message

The Lord has a controversy with his people, and he will contend with Israel. 'O my people, what have I done to you? In what have I wearied you? Answer me! …' 'With what shall I come before the Lord, and bow myself before God on high? Shall I come before him with burnt-offerings, with calves a year old? Will the Lord be pleased with thousands of rams, with tens of thousands of rivers of oil? Shall I give my firstborn for my transgression, the fruit of my body for the sin of my soul?' He has told you, O mortal, what is good; and what does the Lord require of you but to do justice, and to love kindness, and to walk humbly with your God?

Micah envisages a cosmic courtroom scene. The case is God versus his people, to be heard before the mountains and the very foundations of the Earth, the court of the whole creation. It could not be more serious.

God's accusation comes as a question: 'What have I done to you?' God wants to know why the people he has saved and redeemed have found it impossible to respond in faithful commitment.

The answer, they claim, is that they have not known what God wants of them. There is an almost painfully insulting tone as the speaker claims that they did not even know if God required them to sacrifice their firstborn children.

This provokes Micah's definitive statement of God's expectations of his people. They have been told repeatedly. Some versions use the phrase, 'He has shown you what is good'—a reminder that God is not a distant deity who thunders his demands from afar, but one who walks with his people, demonstrating the nature of goodness.

So, here is the core of the prophetic message: do justice, love kindness, walk humbly with God. If that is what God wanted 3000 years ago, you can be certain that it is what God wants now, too. The problem is not in the knowing, but in the doing. Thank God that he gives us his Spirit so that we can live his life of justice and mercy.

Reflection

Are these three separate activities or three aspects of the one activity? How pleased is God if we only attempt one or two of the three?

SR

JEREMIAH 30:1–3, 8–9 (NIV, ABRIDGED)

The hope of freedom

This is the word that came to Jeremiah from the Lord... '"The days are coming... when I will bring my people Israel and Judah back from captivity and restore them to the land I gave to their forefathers to possess... In that day," declares the Lord Almighty, "I will break the yoke off their necks and will tear off their bonds; no longer will foreigners enslave them. Instead, they will serve the Lord their God."'

Just over a year ago I stood in Trafalgar Square, along with 22,000 others, as a frail old man made his way to a podium on the steps in front of the National Gallery. His voice, though, was as strong as ever and he spoke with the clarion call of a prophet: 'But in this new century, millions of people in the world's poorest countries remain imprisoned, enslaved and in chains. They are trapped in the prison of poverty. It is time to set them free.'

As Nelson Mandela made his simple and powerful speech in support of the campaign to 'Make Poverty History', I looked across to where people were gathered on the balconies of South Africa House. This is the embassy of the nation that had once imprisoned the man who became their president and gained a unique global reputation and recognition. Once people had gathered here to call for his freedom; now they heard him call for the freedom of others.

Jeremiah spent a considerable amount of his life in prison, under arrest, with people wishing him dead. Even in the depths of injustice and despair, however, he brought words of hope: the people who would be exiled would also be set free and restored to their rightful position.

True freedom is expressed in the service of God. That's why the task of the prophet was always the same, whether offering hope or bringing warning: to challenge, provoke, inspire so that God's plans and purposes could be fulfilled in lives of service.

Reflection

The resources for today's Women's World Day of Prayer come from South Africa. Nelson Mandela is a symbol of freedom, but still there are millions longing for freedom: freedom from fear, freedom from want, freedom to worship God without threat. Because God has set us free, we can serve him by doing all in our power to set others free.

SR

Tell us pleasant things

Go now, write it on a tablet for them, inscribe it on a scroll, that for the days to come it may be an everlasting witness. These are rebellious people, deceitful children, children unwilling to listen to the Lord's instruction. They say to the seers, 'See no more visions!' and to the prophets, 'Give us no more visions of what is right! Tell us pleasant things, prophesy illusions. Leave this way, get off this path, and stop confronting us with the Holy One of Israel!'... This is what the Sovereign Lord, the Holy One of Israel, says: 'In repentance and rest is your salvation, in quietness and trust is your strength, but you would have none of it.... Yet the Lord longs to be gracious to you; he rises to show you compassion. For the Lord is a God of justice. Blessed are all who wait for him!'

What do you want from a prophet? If someone is going to speak words from God, which words do you want to hear?

Experience suggests that many people need to hear a word that encourages them, because so many live with discouragement, even from their experiences within their churches. Many people need to hear God remind them that they are loved and cherished, because life has created the doubt that they will ever be accepted, loved and cherished.

If you are among these people, then hold on to the promise that God longs to be gracious and show you compassion.

Isaiah also faced people who wanted the illusion of comfort rather than its reality. They did not want a prophet who made them face facts. These people preferred to opt for a moral vacuum rather than be confronted with a Holy God who made demands as to how they behaved: 'Give us no more visions of what is right.'

Their preference was for 'pleasant things'. They wanted to turn the Lion of the tribe of Judah into a domestic cat, but God is a God of justice. He can't deal out favours for the few, but he can set free millions of people to follow him and serve him.

Prayer

Loving Father, grant us the encouragement of the truth of your love, as well as the courage to hear your words of reproof and correction.
Amen

SR

The sign of the sabbath

Then the Lord said to Moses, 'Say to the Israelites, "You must observe my Sabbaths. This will be a sign between me and you for the generations to come, so that you may know that I am the Lord, who makes you holy.... For six days, work is to be done, but the seventh day is a Sabbath of rest, holy to the Lord.... The Israelites are to observe the Sabbath, celebrating it for the generations to come as a lasting covenant. It will be a sign between me and the Israelites for ever, for in six days the Lord made the heavens and the earth, and on the seventh day he abstained from work and rested."'

One wit noted that nostalgia is not what it was. It's also true that Sundays are not what they were. The changes to Sunday observance highlight the wider encroachments of secularism into the fabric of our culture. Not all the changes have been negative: excessive legalism was a genuine stumbling-block to many. Nonetheless, the relentless onslaught of commercialism and the growth of shopping as a major leisure activity mean that our understanding of a day of rest has been drastically redefined.

The Sabbath was instituted by God to be a sign. First, it was a sign of holiness. Because God was holy, there was to be a day for being different, separated out from the rest of the week. It was a day not for lifeless, formal religious observance, but to focus on God and be refreshed in body, mind and spirit.

Second, the Sabbath was a sign of a creation truth: a permanent weekly reminder that work and rest was a pattern revealed in the very creation of the universe. It was not just God's instruction; it was the way God behaved.

Interestingly, the sign was between the people and God, but it is also a reminder that, in our culture, the balance we demonstrate between work and worship, rest and labour is a sign of our view of God and his values.

Sunday reflection

Our church meets in a cinema. We enjoy fellowship after worship in the foyer as people arrive to see a film. As we reclaim a secular space for the holiness of God, we hope that it's a sign of a positive and holistic celebration of life.

SR

Building up

Pursue love and strive for the spiritual gifts, and especially that you may prophesy. For those who speak in a tongue do not speak to other people but to God; for nobody understands them, since they are speaking mysteries in the Spirit. On the other hand, those who prophesy speak to other people for their building up and encouragement and consolation. Those who speak in a tongue build up themselves, but those who prophesy build up the church. Now I would like all of you to speak in tongues, but even more to prophesy. One who prophesies is greater than one who speaks in tongues, unless someone interprets, so that the church may be built up.

I remember the first time that I felt compelled by God's Spirit to speak words of prophecy. It was a large gathering, the first night of a week's conference. A thought arrived in my head and wouldn't go away. I tried to work out how I could know it was from God, not just my own creation. Then, nervously, I decided that it was better to take the risk of letting a potential word from God be heard than to stifle it.

So I said what I felt I had to say and that was that, until a few days later when a young man came and said that my word had been for him—and he had responded. God had spoken and a life had been changed.

Paul emphasizes that the gift of prophecy has a purpose. This was nothing to do with the status or spiritual maturity of the person prophesying—it was all about its impact on the hearers. Building up, encouraging and consoling—anyone contemplating a public prophecy should test it against this criteria. God is not in the business of tearing down or condemning his Church. He is a master builder, not a demolition contractor.

Many still want to debate whether or not God gives the gift of prophecy today. I'll confess that I wish more of this energy were spent building up the Church so that it can serve God in the world. The context for the use of this gift is simple: 'Pursue love' (v. 1).

Prayer

Lord God, pour out your Spirit of prophecy on your Church, so that its members are built up and encouraged as they work for you. Amen

SR

Check it out

And we urge you, brothers, warn those who are idle, encourage the timid, help the weak, be patient with everyone. Make sure that nobody pays back wrong for wrong, but always try to be kind to each other and to everyone else. Be joyful always; pray continually; give thanks in all circumstances, for this is God's will for you in Christ Jesus. Do not put out the Spirit's fire; do not treat prophecies with contempt. Test everything. Hold on to the good. Avoid every kind of evil. May God himself, the God of peace, sanctify you through and through. May your whole spirit, soul and body be kept blameless at the coming of our Lord Jesus Christ.

Isn't it difficult to get the balance right? On the one hand there are Christians who refuse to accept that anyone can have the gift of prophecy in the 21st century, thus rejecting out of hand the possibility that God might have something to say to them through a friend or fellow church member. The supernatural word from God is ruled out.

On the other hand, there are those who claim the most unhelpful and absurd statements as being divinely inspired words of prophecy, causing great hurt and damage if they are taken seriously. What's more, the stories of such disasters are readily repeated by those in the first group, who seize on them as evidence for their conviction that prophecy is a dangerous illusion.

The New Testament indicates that these extremes were not unknown to the apostles as they sought to lead the young Church into a maturity that did not stifle the spirit of God. Paul is very clear that prophetic words are important ('do not treat prophecies with contempt'), but he is equally clear that they have to be tested, so that the hearer can 'hold on to the good'.

This passage reveals the balance of the healthy life: the great virtues of fellowship with other people—patience, kindness, encouragement—are supplemented by the awareness and openness to God that comes from refusing to put out the Spirit's fire. Living that way is good for the whole spirit, soul and body (v. 23).

Prayer

Lord, grant me the gift of discernment so that I can hear your voice amid the noise of life. Amen

SR

Take in... and speak out

'You must speak my words to them, whether they listen or fail to listen, for they are rebellious. But you, son of man, listen to what I say to you. Do not rebel like that rebellious house; open your mouth and eat what I give you.' Then I looked, and I saw a hand stretched out to me. In it was a scroll, which he unrolled before me. On both sides of it were written words of lament and mourning and woe.... Then he said to me, 'Son of man, eat this scroll I am giving you and fill your stomach with it.' So I ate it, and it tasted as sweet as honey in my mouth. He then said to me: 'Son of man, go now to the house of Israel and speak my words to them.'

A truly graphic picture of the prophet's task is presented by this passage! Ezekiel was under orders and simply had to speak out the words God gave to him. Before he could speak out, however, he had to take in.

The words that he was given were not appetizing: 'lament and mourning and woe' does not seem very palatable. However, when Ezekiel responded in obedience, he discovered that God's words were fulfilling and full of sweetness.

It is easy for the Bible to seem forbidding and opaque, even threatening. The purpose of these notes is to make our daily 'snack' nourishing and tasty. It should act as an appetizer for the full meal, when we feast on the revelation of God in Jesus Christ.

That kind of nourishment is essential preparation for those who want to speak out God's word. The equation works the other way, too—those who give time to take in God's word must be ready to speak it out. It is all too easy to see Bible study as an end in itself. We may be impressed by people who know their Bible through and through, but God is only impressed by those who know Jesus and live out the message of the Bible.

Prayer

Loving Father, grant us the ability to digest your word, so that it nourishes all our existence and prompts us to speak out for you and declare what is in your heart. Amen

SR

Listening and hearing

The Lord sent Nathan to David. When he came to him, he said, 'There were two men in a certain town, one rich and the other poor.... Now a traveller came to the rich man, but the rich man refrained from taking one of his own sheep or cattle to prepare a meal.... Instead, he took the ewe lamb that belonged to the poor man and prepared it for the one who had come to him.' David burned with anger against the man and said to Nathan, 'As surely as the Lord lives, the man who did this deserves to die!' ... Then Nathan said to David, 'You are the man! This is what the Lord, the God of Israel, says: "... Why did you despise the word of the Lord by doing what is evil in his eyes?"'... Then David said to Nathan, 'I have sinned against the Lord.'

The story of David touches the heights and plumbs the depths. One who was a man after God's own heart (Acts 13:22) was also capable of arranging the death of a fellow soldier so that he could steal his wife (see 2 Samuel 11). Human beings are capable of great artistic creativity and awful moral depravity—and David was no different.

Nathan the prophet had a task, one he could not have relished. Standing before the powerful to point out their failures is not the best option for a stress-free life. So Nathan uses the oblique approach. His story draws in listeners and engages them in the moral judgment. That's when Nathan feels ready to make his point—and does so, with great force and courage.

Notice how David reacts. He hears the word of God from the prophet. He recognizes his failing and accepts the rebuke. He is filled with remorse and actively seeks God in repentance. Nathan must have been relieved—and encouraged. He had fulfilled his task and done so effectively.

I was once drawn into a similar situation when one of my friends felt it right to confront another with his failings before God in relation to his behaviour towards fellow Christians. I certainly did not relish taking on this task myself, but I was deeply grateful that my friend took this prophetic initiative as we saw him repent and his life change.

Reflection

How ready are we to receive a word of rebuke or correction?

SR

MATTHEW 24:1–5, 35–36 (NRSV)

Signs of the end

As Jesus came out of the temple and was going away, his disciples came to point out to him the buildings of the temple. Then he asked them, 'You see all these, do you not? Truly I tell you, not one stone will be left here upon another; all will be thrown down.' When he was sitting on the Mount of Olives, the disciples came to him privately, saying, 'Tell us, when will this be, and what will be the sign of your coming and of the end of the age?' Jesus answered them, 'Beware that no one leads you astray. For many will come in my name, saying, "I am the Messiah!"... Heaven and earth will pass away, but my words will not pass away. But about that day and hour no one knows, neither the angels of heaven, nor the Son, but only the Father.'

It is all too easy to turn prophecy into fortune-telling. We would love to know about the future—our future. The disciples wanted Jesus to let them in on the secret: when would the world end? To be fair, their interest was not about fear and doom so much as the coming of the King and the Kingdom in glorious reality.

Jesus does not answer the question. Instead, he warns them about being led astray by false prophets, by those whose words are not from God, however plausible and convincing they might seem. As D.A. Carson puts it, 'Empty-headed credulity is as great an enemy of true faith as chronic scepticism' (*NIV Bible Commentary*, Zondervan, 1994).

One of the recurring features of Christian experience in every generation is the insistence on ignoring these words of Jesus and searching the Bible for convincing proof of the date of his return. He said that even he did not know the time, yet countless of his followers have embarrassed themselves and dishonoured their faith by falsely predicting the time and the date.

The important thing is not when Jesus will come, but whether or not we are living in the light of his return. That has been an injunction for 2000 years and it is just as relevant today as it ever was.

Reflection

'Therefore you also must be ready, for the Son of Man is coming at an unexpected hour' (Matthew 24:44).

SR

The life-giving vision

'As the rain and the snow come down from heaven, and do not return to it without watering the earth and making it bud and flourish, so that it yields seed for the sower and bread for the eater, so is my word that goes out from my mouth: It will not return to me empty, but will accomplish what I desire and achieve the purpose for which I sent it. You will go out in joy and be led forth in peace; the mountains and hills will burst into song before you, and all the trees of the field will clap their hands. Instead of the thornbush will grow the pine tree, and instead of briars the myrtle will grow. This will be for the Lord's renown, for an everlasting sign, which will not be destroyed.'

Old Testament prophets could have a hard time of it. Thrown into prison, ignored, losing their families, prompted to let their whole lives become a message from God —it was not a job option for the faint-hearted.

Isaiah was sustained by two things. First, there was the promise from God that he was not wasting his time. God's word, delivered by the prophet, would not be without effect. It would accomplish God's purposes. There must have been days when this promise was the key to Isaiah's perseverance in the task.

The second pillar of his continuing ministry was that God gave him a vision of the future that he could share with others for their inspiration and encouragement. As we read elsewhere, 'Where there is no vision, the people perish' (Proverbs 29:18, KJV). Isaiah repeatedly holds out the grand vision of the God who intervenes in human history, transforming society into a community of fruitfulness and peace. In fact, the whole created order shares in this glorious reality—aren't you longing to see the trees clapping their hands?

Proverbs 29:18 reads differently in another version: 'Where there is no prophecy, the people cast off restraint' (NRSV). The word translated as 'vision' above also means 'prophecy'. To the prophet is granted the vision—the ability to see as God sees—and the privilege of communicating it to others.

Prayer

Lord, thank you for the inspiration of your vision of the future. In your mercy, grant that I may experience its fulfilment. Amen

SR

Don't forget to renew your annual subscription to *New Daylight*! If you enjoy the notes, why not also consider giving a gift subscription to a friend or member of your family?

You will find a subscription order form overleaf.

New Daylight is also available from your local Christian bookshop.

❏ I would like to take out a subscription myself (complete your name and address details only once)

❏ I would like to give a gift subscription (please complete both name and address sections below)

Your name _____

Your address _____

_____

_____Postcode _____

Gift subscription name _____

Gift subscription address _____

_____

_____Postcode _____

Please send *New Daylight* beginning with the May / September 2006 / January 07 issue: (delete as applicable)

(please tick box)	UK	SURFACE	AIR MAIL
NEW DAYLIGHT	❏ £12.00	❏ £13.35	❏ £15.60
NEW DAYLIGHT 3-year sub	❏ £29.55		
NEW DAYLIGHT LARGE PRINT	❏ £16.80	❏ £20.40	❏ £24.90

Please complete the payment details below and send your coupon, with appropriate payment, to: **BRF, First Floor, Elsfield Hall, 15–17 Elsfield Way, Oxford OX2 8FG.**

Total enclosed £ _____ (cheques should be made payable to 'BRF')

Payment by cheque ❏ postal order ❏ Visa ❏ Mastercard ❏ Switch ❏

Card number: ⬚⬚⬚⬚⬚⬚⬚⬚⬚⬚⬚⬚⬚⬚⬚⬚⬚⬚⬚⬚⬚⬚

Expiry date of card: ⬚⬚⬚⬚   Issue number (Switch): ⬚⬚⬚⬚

Signature (essential if paying by credit/Switch card) _____

❏ Please do not send me further information about BRF publications.

BRF resources are available from your local Christian bookshop. BRF is a Registered Charity

Cuthbert of Lindisfarne

There are some saints whom you can admire, but rather at arm's length; there are others who become friends and companions on the journey. For me, Cuthbert is one of the friends and companions. Perhaps it's partly because he came from my part of the world—from southern Scotland and northern England. Born in what are now the Scottish borders, around 634, he spent his entire life there and in northern England.

I share the same way of life that he chose—life in a religious community, praying and working together. I know that if I could be transported back to his times, everything would be strange—the language, landscape, politics, food, church life. The seventh century was a time when Christianity was very new in the British islands. Many areas were still largely pagan, priests and churches were few and widely scattered and much of the life of the Church centred on the monasteries. Politically, there was no England or Scotland, but a number of small kingdoms, often at odds with each other.

Cuthbert was obviously very capable as he was made guest brother of Melrose, the monastery he joined aged 17, while still young, then prior of Melrose and, later, of Lindisfarne, on its semi-island off the Northumbria coast, and, finally, bishop of Lindisfarne. He also had a strong call to prayer and lived this out in periods of solitude. His solitude was never total, however. People valued his wisdom greatly and would travel even to his isolated hermitage on Farne, an island south of Lindisfarne, to ask for advice and prayers.

He had gifts of healing and prophecy and there are many stories of him healing people both in his lifetime and after his death. These are found in the only sources we have for his life—two biographies. One was written by a monk on Lindisfarne around 700, only a few years after Cuthbert's death in 687, while the other is by the Venerable Bede, written in the early part of the eighth century. Both contain vivid pictures of Cuthbert's life and ministry, but we have no words from Cuthbert himself—he left no writings. However, in pilgrimage to the places he knew—to Lindisfarne and to Durham in particular—it is still possible in some way to encounter him and be led by his example to be nearer to the God he served and worshipped.

Helen Julian CSF

PSALM 74:1, 4–7, 12 (NRSV)

A sacred place

O God, why do you cast us off for ever? Why does your anger smoke against the sheep of your pasture?... Your foes have roared within your holy place; they set up their emblems there. At the upper entrance they hacked the wooden trellis with axes. And then, with hatchets and hammers, they smashed all its carved work. They set your sanctuary on fire; they desecrated the dwelling-place of your name, bringing it to the ground.... Yet God my King is from of old, working salvation in the earth.

On 8 June 793, on the north-east coast of England, something terrifying happened. Viking invaders attacked the monastery on Lindisfarne, killing some of the monks and making off with many of the treasures of the monastery.

Alcuin, a contemporary writer, lamented the raid, calling Lindisfarne 'a place more sacred than any other in Britain'. Perhaps the monks felt that God had abandoned them, as the psalmist did, lamenting the destruction of his holy place.

Yet, what really mattered was what had made the place holy. For the psalmist, it was that this was 'the dwelling place of your name'; for the monks it was that Lindisfarne had been the home of Cuthbert for much of his life and that he had been buried there. Many relics associated with him— clothing, hair, leather from the walls of his hermitage on Farne Island— were also on the island and helped to draw the pilgrims who came to pray to him and seek healing.

In the end, it was these holy things that the monks valued and so when the Viking raids continued, the community moved Cuthbert's body and the relics to the Northumberland mainland for a time. They returned to Lindisfarne, but, when a new wave of invasions threatened, in 875, they left for good, wandering for seven years before settling in Chester-le-Street. There they lived peacefully for over a century, but in 995 the Viking threat returned. They fled south for a time and, on the way back to Chester-le-Street, turned aside to Durham, where today it is still possible to visit Cuthbert's shrine and see some of the relics that the monks preserved.

Sunday reflection

Where are your sacred places? If you had to leave, what would you take with you?

HJ CSF

Signs of glory

In that region there were shepherds living in the fields, keeping watch over their flock by night. Then an angel of the Lord stood before them, and the glory of the Lord shone around them, and they were terrified. But the angel said to them, 'Do not be afraid; for see—I am bringing you good news of great joy for all the people: to you is born this day in the city of David a Saviour, who is the Messiah, the Lord…. When the angels had left them and gone into heaven, the shepherds said to one another, 'Let us go now to Bethlehem and see this thing that has taken place, which the Lord has made known to us.'

Cuthbert would have found this passage familiar. He too was a shepherd as a young man and took his turn watching the flock by night. He used to make use of the quiet hours of darkness to pray. It was while praying that he saw something that changed his life.

Suddenly, the darkness was lit up by streams of light, and he had a vison of angels escorting a bright human soul to heaven. The next day, he heard that Aidan, bishop of Lindisfarne, and originally a monk from Iona, had died at the time he saw the vision. Cuthbert took the sheep back to their owner and set off to join the monastery at Melrose.

Like the shepherds near Bethlehem, he was moved to action by his vision of God—'let us go… and see'—although it's interesting to note that neither the shepherds nor Cuthbert were given direct instructions about what to do; they had to interpret what they'd seen. God rarely issues unmistakable instructions; far more often he shows us something of himself, and leaves us free to decide how to respond.

Others, too, will play their part in finding out God's will for us. When Cuthbert arrived at Melrose, the prior, Boisil, had an intuition that this boy (Cuthbert was about 17) would be a saint. He, too, was tuned in to God and the signs of God's presence and work around him.

Prayer

Gracious God, open my eyes to the signs of your glory around me and open my heart and mind so I can interpret your call and follow it with boldness.

HJ CSF

Making disciples

Now the 11 disciples went to Galilee, to the mountain to which Jesus had directed them. When they saw him, they worshipped him; but some doubted. And Jesus came and said to them, 'All authority in heaven and on earth has been given to me. Go therefore and make disciples of all nations, baptizing them in the name of the Father and of the Son and of the Holy Spirit, and teaching them to obey everything that I have commanded you. And remember, I am with you always, to the end of the age.'

One of my favourite relics at Durham Cathedral is a small portable altar, about 13cm square, made of oak. It is decorated with five crosses and a Latin inscription in honour of Peter. Cuthbert would have taken it with him as he travelled outside the monastery, so that he could celebrate the eucharist wherever he went. This would have been part of his missionary work, for which he had a great passion.

The monks of Cuthbert's day did not just stay within their monasteries, waiting for people to come to them, but went out, like the early disciples of Jesus, to make others into disciples. Christianity was still new and fragile in Britain and many people had yet to hear the gospel. So, even before Cuthbert was ordained as a priest, he made many journeys, preaching the gospel to those who had not yet heard it and instructing and encouraging those who had already become Christians. Faith was not well-rooted and, particularly in times of danger or difficulty, such as plague, there was a great temptation to return to previous pagan practices.

Cuthbert had a particular concern for the places neglected by others because of their remoteness, poverty or squalor and would spend two or three weeks at a time living there with the people. He rarely went on these journeys alone—he took one or more companions, usually fellow monks—so that, in a sense, the monastery came to the people. They continued their times of prayer together and so taught by their example as well as by their words.

Reflection

Who are the people around you who might hear the gospel through you? What inspiration for evangelism can you find in Cuthbert and his fellow monks?

HJ CSF

Acts 9:36–42 (NRSV)

Faith to be made whole

Now in Joppa there was a disciple whose name was Tabitha.... She was devoted to good works and acts of charity. At that time she became ill and died... The disciples... sent two men to him [Peter] with the request, 'Please come to us without delay.' So Peter got up and went with them; and when he arrived, they took him to the room upstairs... He knelt down and prayed. He turned to the body and said 'Tabitha, get up.' Then she opened her eyes, and seeing Peter, she sat up. He gave her his hand and helped her up... This became known throughout Joppa and many believed in the Lord.

Cuthbert followed the example of Jesus' early disciples in his preaching and making of disciples, as well as healing. The Acts of the Apostles contains a number of healing stories, as do the Gospels of course. Like Jesus and the apostles, Cuthbert sometimes healed directly, using prayer, laying on of hands and holy oil or water. At other times, healing took place at a distance, via something that he had touched.

A common factor in all the stories is faith. Cuthbert's biographers are determined to distinguish the healing offered by the Christian God from that which pagan gods could offer.

One of Cuthbert's friends, Aelflaed, abbess of the monastery at Whitby, had a long illness. She wished for something of Cuthbert's, as she believed that she would be cured by it. Soon afterwards, a linen sash arrived from Cuthbert. She wrapped it around herself and was completely cured. One of her nuns was also cured of excruciating pains in the head. The sash then disappeared. Bede says that this was to prevent people flocking to it for healing. If some were lacking in faith and so were not cured, they would have doubted Cuthbert's sanctity.

Miracles were seen as a sign that their worker was favoured by God and, in a world of pagan magic (and no modern medicine), were a powerful tool of evangelism. However, their context was always one of faith—faith in the Christian God on the part of the healer, the healed and those who cared for the sick person.

Prayer

God of wholeness, give me faith in healing, for myself and for others.

HJ CSF

Words of truth

[The Lord said to Moses]: 'I will raise up for them a prophet like you from among their own people; I will put my words in the mouth of the prophet, who shall speak to them everything that I command. Anyone who does not heed the words that the prophet shall speak in my name, I myself shall hold accountable.... You may say to yourself, "How can we recognize a word that the Lord has not spoken?" If a prophet speaks in the name of the Lord but the thing does not take place or prove true, it is a word that the Lord has not spoken. The prophet has spoken it presumptuously; do not be frightened by it.'

As a healer, Cuthbert echoes much in the New Testament; as a prophet, there is a strong connection to the Old Testament. Like the Old Testament prophets, Cuthbert works in a number of different spheres. Sometimes the prophecy is for one individual. During a time of plague, Cuthbert visited a village to comfort the people. There he met a woman—one of her sons had already died and the other was dying in her arms. Cuthbert blessed the boy and promised his mother that he would live and this prophecy proved true.

Sometimes the prophecy was on a larger, more political scale. As bishop, Cuthbert travelled to Carlisle, where King Ecgfrith had gone to fight against the Picts. Ecgfrith's queen was staying in her sister's convent in Carlisle and Cuthbert went to support her in this time of crisis. While being shown round Carlisle, he had a sudden premonition that, at that moment, the battle was being decided and the outcome would not be good. Two days later, a messenger arrived and at the very moment that Cuthbert had had the premonition, the king and all his bodyguards had been slaughtered by the enemy.

Cuthbert also foresaw his own death and warned a hermit friend, Hereberht, who used to come to him for counsel, that this would be their last meeting.

Cuthbert's prophetic gifts were another sign of God's favour and that God chose to work through him in many different spheres of his life.

Prayer

God of the prophets, help me to listen to your words in the mouths of others and to hear when I should speak it.

HJ CSF

Patterns of holiness

On the third day there was a wedding in Cana of Galilee, and the mother of Jesus was there. Jesus and his disciples had also been invited to the wedding. When the wine gave out, the mother of Jesus said to him, 'They have no wine.' … Jesus said to [the servants], 'Fill the jars with water.' And they filled them up to the brim. He said to them, 'Now draw some out, and take it to the chief steward.' So they took it. When the steward tasted the water that had become wine… [he] called the bridegroom and said to him… 'you have kept the good wine until now.'

Perhaps you have already noticed some marked similarities between the stories of Cuthbert and stories in the Bible? The story of the wedding at Cana has its own parallel in his life, too. Cuthbert was visiting the convent at Tynemouth. He asked for water, blessed it and drank a little, then passed the cup on. Those who drank from it thought it the best wine that they had ever tasted.

The story of the sash sent to Aelflaed echoes the handkerchiefs touched by Paul (Acts 19:11–12) that have healing powers. There are many more echoes—of Elijah when Cuthbert is provided with food while on a journey and healings from demon possession, to name just two. His biographers don't try to hide these similarities-indeed, often they point them out themselves, by direct quotation from the Bible or allusion to it. This is a kind of writing where originality doesn't seem important as certain stories are copied almost word for word from one life of a saint to another. What is going on here?

There's a clue in the proper name for lives of saints—they are not biographies, but hagiographies. They are not primarily history, but theology. Their purpose is not to recount all the individual details of the saint's life, but to show that God was working in him or her, as he had done in the people we read about in the Bible. So, Cuthbert's hagiographers used the stories from scripture that were at the heart of their own faith as templates for the stories of Cuthbert, as guarantees of his authenticity.

Reflection

Can you see places in your own life that echo stories in scripture?

HJ CSF

Dissension and debate

Then certain individuals came down from Judea and were teaching the brothers, 'Unless you are circumcised according to the custom of Moses, you cannot be saved.' And after Paul and Barnabas had no small dissension and debate with them, Paul and Barnabas and some of the others were appointed to go up to Jerusalem to discuss this question with the apostles and the elders.... When they came to Jerusalem, they were welcomed by the church and the apostles and the elders, and they reported all that God had done with them.... The apostles and the elders met together to consider this matter.

'Dissension and debate' have been part of the life of the Church from the beginning and Cuthbert was not exempt. When he first came to Lindisfarne as prior, not all the brothers welcomed him and he had quite a struggle to bring them round to the changes he wanted to make.

The big debate in his time was about the date of Easter. There were two different ways of calculating it —one followed by Rome and the churches influenced by it and another followed by Ireland and the churches influenced by it. In northern England at Cuthbert's time, these two influences met. In fact, the royal household itself was divided, as the king kept the Irish date and his queen, from Kent, the Roman one. It can seem a very petty quarrel, but both sides thought that they were being faithful to the tradition of the Church and were reluctant to give way.

In 664, a synod was called at Whitby to decide the matter. Bishops, priests, monks and nuns came from far and wide to debate with each other. Oswy, king of Northumbria, in the end gave judgment for the Roman side and most of those present accepted this decision. However, some could not and it was many years before all the churches followed the Roman practice. Colman, bishop of Lindisfarne at the time of the synod and leader of the Irish side, resigned and returned to Scotland rather than follow the Roman practice.

Reflection

What issues in the Church concern you at present? Are you willing to keep talking to those with whom you disagree and accept that you may be the one who has to change?

HJ CSF

Sunday 19 March

1 KINGS 17:2–6 (NRSV)

Gifts of solitude

The word of the Lord came to him [Elijah], saying, 'Go from here and turn eastwards, and hide yourself by the Wadi Cherith, which is east of the Jordan. You shall drink from the wadi, and I have commanded the ravens to feed you there.' So he went and did according to the word of the Lord; he went and lived by the Wadi Cherith, which is east of the Jordan. The ravens brought him bread and meat in the morning, and bread and meat in the evening, and he drank from the wadi.

Cuthbert had always been drawn to solitude (remember earlier I mentioned his night-time prayer as a young shepherd?), but as he grew older he desired it more and more. He was given permission to spend time on a very small tidal island just off the coast of Lindisfarne, near to the monastery and then to move to an even more remote place. This was Inner Farne, which is a true island, with more than a mile of sea between it and the mainland. Here he built a simple hermitage with an oratory for prayer and a hut to live in.

To begin with his brothers kept him supplied with food, but then Cuthbert decided to grow his own. He asked them to bring him tools and seed and successfully grew barley, but birds came down and began to eat it. Cuthbert questioned the birds, asking them why they were eating what someone else had grown, but accepted that their need might be greater than his. The birds flew off and did no further damage.

Cuthbert seems to have had an especially close relationship with birds, especially in his solitude. Another story tells of ravens that he found taking straw from the roof of one of his buildings to make their nests. He rebuked them and they flew off. However, one returned three days later and stood before Cuthbert, with its wings spread and its head bowed low, to express its apology. Cuthbert forgave them all and the raven then returned with a gift—a piece of pig's lard. Cuthbert kept it and would offer it to his visitors to grease their shoes with. Thus, solitude brought Cuthbert closer not only to God but also God's creation.

Sunday reflection

What gifts does solitude bring to you? How do you share them with your community?

HJ CSF

Whenever you pray

And whenever you pray, do not be like the hypocrites: for they love to stand and pray in the synagogues and at the street corners, so that they may be seen by others. Truly I tell you, they have received their reward. But whenever you pray, go into your room and shut the door and pray to your Father who is in secret; and your Father who sees in secret will reward you. When you are praying, do not heap up empty phrases as the Gentiles do; for they think that they will be heard because of their many words. Do not be like them, for your Father knows what you need before you ask him.

Above everything else, it was his desire for prayer that drew Cuthbert to solitude. As a monk, he was committed to regular times of prayer with his brothers, several times a day, but he also prayed alone, sometimes staying up at night to do so. It was common for monks to know the entire psalter by heart and Cuthbert would pray the psalms as he walked round Lindisfarne when he was prior, doing the rounds of his monks and helping in their work.

His regular life of prayer continued when he was away from the monastery, too. Once, when he was visiting the nuns at Colding-ham, at the request of the abbess, he rose in the middle of the night and went down to the beach to pray. One of the monks who had accompanied him followed him in secret. He saw Cuthbert walk out into the sea and stand praying, up to his chest in the cold water. At daybreak, Cuthbert returned to the beach, where he knelt down and continued his prayers. Two otters came out of the water and tried to dry his feet with their fur and warm them with their breath. Cuthbert blessed them when they had finished and then he returned to the convent in time for morning prayer.

It seems right to have this story on the day when the Church celebrates Cuthbert as prayer was the mainspring of his life. It fuelled all his other activities and seems to have been his 'default setting'.

Prayer

Loving God, give me a desire for prayer like Cuthbert's and let his prayers aid me on his special day.

HJ CSF

1 Timothy 3:1–3, 6–7 (NRSV)

Serving the Church

The saying is sure: whoever aspires to the office of bishop desires a noble task. Now a bishop must be above reproach, married only once, temperate, sensible, respectable, hospitable, an apt teacher, not a drunkard, not violent but gentle, not quarrelsome, and not a lover of money…. He must not be a recent convert, or he may be puffed up with conceit and fall into the condemnation of the devil. Moreover, he must be well thought of by outsiders, so that he may not fall into disgrace and the snare of the devil.

Cuthbert hoped to spend the rest of his life as a hermit, but it was not to be. A synod of the Church—traditionally thought to have taken place at Alnmouth—elected him bishop of Lindisfarne. At first he refused to accept, but when the king, Ecgfrith, and the bishop, Trumwine, with a whole group of others, sailed to Farne and begged him with tears to accept, he, also with tears, consented. Perhaps it was not entirely a surprise—Boisil, his first prior at Melrose, had prophesied Cuthbert's future to him and had hinted that he would be a bishop.

Once consecrated, he threw himself into the work. He travelled around his large diocese, preaching and teaching, baptizing and confirming, healing and caring for those in need. At the same time, he remained a monk, living simply. Usually he travelled with a number of fellow monks, with whom he prayed the daily offices, so, in a sense, the monastery travelled with him. Often they went to places where there was no church building, so had to live in tents and preach and worship in the open air.

He was equally available to the rich and the poor. We have already seen how he prophesied the death in battle of the king. There are also many healing stories from this part of his life, including members of the king's bodyguard—one of whom became a monk himself and told the story to Bede—a sister belonging to a very small community of nuns and a young man from a very remote mountain area, brought to him during a confirmation service.

Reflection

What do you think are the most important qualities that should be possessed by leaders in the Church? How do you yourself exercise leadership?

HJ CSF

Solitary conflict

Put on the whole armour of God, so that you may be able to stand against the wiles of the devil. For our struggle is not against enemies of blood and flesh, but against the rulers, against the authorities, against the cosmic powers of this present darkness, against the spiritual forces of evil in the heavenly places. Therefore take up the whole armour of God, so that you may be able to withstand on that evil day, and having done everything, to stand firm.

After two years as a bishop, Cuthbert resigned and returned to the life of a hermit on Farne. Bede refers to 'his beloved life of solitary conflict' and this hints at another dimension of the life. It was not just a peaceful communing with God in a beautiful place, but a way of engaging with the forces of darkness, in a spiritual warfare.

From early on in Cuthbert's ministry he had been aware of these forces. On one of his preaching journeys from Melrose, it seems, fire broke out in the village houses while he preached—a fire that could not be quenched by water but only by his prayers. He spoke of this as a distraction sent by the devil.

Farne itself was thought to be haunted by devils and Cuthbert was the first person brave enough to try to live there alone. Bede uses the imagery of Ephesians 6 to describe how, as a soldier of God, he took over the island for God, but it was not a once and for all victory. Bede records Cuthbert saying, 'How often have the demons tried to cast me headlong from yonder rock; how often have they hurled stones as if to kill me; with one fantastic temptation after another they have sought to disillusion me into retreating from this battlefield; but they have never yet succeeded in harming either soul or body, nor do they terrify me' (Bede: Life of Cuthbert 22, in *The Age of Bede*, Penguin, 1965).

You may notice the echoes of the temptation of Christ in this story (Luke 4:5–13); Cuthbert, like Christ, took evil seriously, but also knew that in Christ it had been overcome.

Prayer

God of goodness, keep me safe from all evil and make me bold to fight it in your name.

HJ CSF

Dying in Christ

Return, O my soul, to your rest, for the Lord has dealt bountifully with you. For you have delivered my soul from death, from eyes from tears, my feet from stumbling. I walk before the Lord in the land of the living.... What shall I return to the Lord for all his bounty to me? I will lift up the cup of salvation and call on the name of the Lord, I will pay my vows to the Lord in the presence of all his people. Precious in the sight of the Lord is the death of his faithful ones. O Lord, I am your servant; I am your servant, the child of your serving-maid. You have loosed my bonds.

Cuthbert did not have long to enjoy the solitude of Farne again after the busyness of his life as a bishop. Before long he fell ill, an illness that lasted for three weeks. His brothers knew that he was dying and begged to be allowed to stay with him and care for him, but Cuthbert refused. He wanted to be alone and told them that God would show them when to return. A storm prevented them for reaching the island for five days, so they kept a constant vigil of prayer during those days. Cuthbert, too, was praying. When the storm abated and they returned to Farne, they found him very weak and drained, having suffered both physically and spiritually, in a final conflict with the powers of darkness.

Now Cuthbert was willing to be cared for and several brothers stayed on Farne with him, while others visited. He was in the small guest house near the landing place but, when he knew that he was about to die, he asked to be taken back to the hermitage. Too weak to walk, he was carried by his brothers. Herefrith, who told the story of Cuthbert's death to Bede, stayed with him now. Cuthbert continued to pray and at the time of night prayer he received Communion. Then, raising his eyes and his hands to heaven and praising God, he died. It was 20 March 687.

Prayer

O God of life and death, keep me faithful in your service and joyful in your praise all the days of my life, and all the hours of my death.

HJ CSF

Words from God

Now in the church at Antioch there were prophets and teachers: Barnabas, Simeon who was called Niger, Lucius of Cyrene, Manaen a member of the court of Herod the ruler, and Saul. While they were worshipping the Lord and fasting, the Holy Spirit said, 'Set apart for me Barnabas and Saul for the work to which I have called them.' Then after fasting and praying they laid their hands on them and sent them off.

After his death, Cuthbert's body was taken to Lindisfarne, where with great reverence it was buried in the monastery church, near to that of Aidan, whose death had sparked Cuthbert's vocation. Very soon, pilgrims began to flock to the island. Eleven years after his death, the monks received permission to put Cuthbert's bones in a lighter coffin above ground, so that they could be better venerated. To their amazement, when they opened the coffin, they found that his body had not decayed and seemed not to be dead but sleeping. This was taken as a clear sign of his sanctity and increased the reputation of the shrine. It was around this time that the famous Lindisfarne Gospels were made on the island, by Eadfrith, who was bishop at the time.

As we have seen, however, even Cuthbert's reputation did not save Lindisfarne from the Viking raids. When the monks finally left in 875, they became wanderers and then settled in Chester-le-street. It was while returning there in 995 after a brief journey south to escape renewed Viking raids that Durham became part of the story.

As they travelled, the cart on which Cuthbert's body was being transported became immovable. They felt that this was a message from Cuthbert and held a three-day fast and vigil of prayer to find out what he wanted. A man named Eadmer received a revelation that Cuthbert wanted to rest in Durham, a small settlement in a bend of the River Wear, and so they took the body there and built a temporary wooden church, soon replaced by a stone cathedral.

More than 300 years after his death, Cuthbert was still powerfully active and present to those who revered him. He appeared to have chosen his own final resting place, the place where he remains today.

Reflection

Have you a saint to whom you feel particularly close?

HJ CSF

Pilgrim places

I was glad when they said to me, 'Let us go to the house of Lord!'
Our feet are standing within your gates, O Jerusalem. Jerusalem—
built as a city that is bound firmly together. To it the tribes go up,
the tribes of the Lord, as was decreed for Israel, to give thanks to
the name of the Lord. For there the thrones for judgement were set
up, the thrones of the house of David. Pray for the peace of
Jerusalem: 'May they prosper who love you. Peace be within your
walls, and security within your towers.'

It was in Durham, at the shrine of Cuthbert behind the high altar in the great Norman cathedral, that I first encountered him. The shrine is where it has been for centuries, though it is now simple—just a slab in the floor with Cuthbert's name on it. Before the Reformation it was very different—made of green marble, decorated with gold and with a covering, scarlet inside and gilded and painted outside. It was raised at certain times and there were six silver bells on one of the ropes that raised it so that people knew when this was happening. It had four seats by it where the sick could kneel or lean. It was one of the main centres of pilgrimage in England for centuries and became very rich as a result of the gifts given by grateful pilgrims.

The physical surroundings don't really matter; what matters is the presence of holiness, and that is unmistakable. Just as the Old Testament pilgrims to Jerusalem found it a place of God's special presence, so it is in other places of pilgrimage today.

Many pilgrims still come to Lindisfarne to find the God whom Cuthbert served there and to honour Aidan, Cuthbert and others who gave their lives in that place.

However, as the people of the Old Testament found, God can be known not only in Jerusalem, and not only by his chosen people, but everywhere and by everyone and so can his saints. Pilgrimage places help us to meet them, but in some way they come with us when we leave and can be our companions every day.

Prayer

May I draw closer to you, God, through the example and companionship of Cuthbert.

HJ CSF

Revelation 15—18

It must be admitted that the book of Revelation is difficult to understand. Because it has been used as a 'happy hunting ground' by those who seek to perpetuate weird and unhelpful doctrines, many choose to ignore it and concentrate instead on parts of the Bible that are easier and less challenging. This is a pity because, although they sound strange to modern ears, the warnings and encouragement that John conveyed to Christians in Asia Minor are still relevant. They face the realities of contemporary power struggles and confront them with the power of God as it is seen in the death and resurrection of Christ.

In exile on Patmos, John had a vision in which the risen Christ told him to 'write in a book... what you have seen, what is, and what is to take place after this' (see Revelation 1:10–19). Revelation was written towards the close of the reign of the Emperor Domitian (AD91–63), when he began to insist that his subjects worship his image and refer to him as 'Lord and God'. Many Christians suffered martyrdom for refusing to do so.

As apocalyptic writing, Revelation is full of symbolism, with strange beasts, significant numbers and tumultuous happenings. Using the dramatic language of visions, it looks forward to the end of the world. All must face judgment, but beyond is the promise of a new heaven and a new Earth. The symbolic language prevented the authorities from realizing that the book was a trumpet call to the persecuted to resist evil, stand firm in their faith and confront the worship of idols. It assured them that, beyond the worst that Rome could do, God reigned supreme and Christ's resurrection had won the decisive victory over evil.

No other New Testament writing has as many references to such a wide range of Old Testament texts and concepts. Revelation has been described as a 'rereading of the Old Testament in the light of Christ' and 'prophecy staged in eternity'.

Chapters 15—18 begin with a celebration of the victory of God, then show the reality of judgment. In the vision of seven angels with bowls from which they poured plagues on the earth, we see the conquest of all that is opposed to Christ. 'Babylon', the anti-Christian empire, and the 'Beast' or 'Antichrist' are destroyed. Christians are assured of eternal life and the final divine triumph is celebrated.

Peter Graves

REVELATION 15:2–4 (NRSV)

Stand firm and claim the victory

And I saw what appeared to be a sea of glass mixed with fire, and those who had conquered the beast... standing beside the sea of glass with harps of God in their hands. And they sing the song of Moses, the servant of God, and the song of the Lamb: 'Great and amazing are your deeds, Lord God the Almighty! Just and true are your ways, King of the nations! Lord, who will not fear and glorify your name? For you alone are holy. All nations will come and worship before you, for your judgments have been revealed.'

The key to understanding this passage—and, indeed, the whole of the book of Revelation—is the song of Moses and of the Lamb, which is sung by 'those who had conquered the beast'. In an age of persecution, struggling churches would have been greatly encouraged as John reminded them that evil powers opposed to God's purpose of salvation could never win the day. Multitudes of the faithful, by remaining loyal to Christ, had already passed the test and won a great victory against evil of every kind.

The songs of Moses are recorded in Exodus 15 and Deuteronomy 32. They celebrate his leading the Hebrews from slavery in Egypt through the Red Sea and the wilderness, towards the freedom of the promised land. By linking the exodus with the resurrection victory of Christ the Lamb, John wants to emphasize that liberation is now happening on a cosmic scale as people are released from the slavery of sin. The exodus story, therefore, has universal significance. The 'sea of glass' has become a kind of heavenly Red Sea. Just as Pharaoh and his army perished in the sea, so the beast and his allies will be overthrown. Through the redemption of Christ, the victors over the beast have been delivered from their would be destroyers and stand in the presence of God.

God is praised for his marvellous deeds and just ways. His holiness will attract all nations to worship him and willingly submit to his lordship.

Sunday prayer

When the going gets tough, Lord, help me to realize that, in Christ, the ultimate victory is already won and therefore evil never has the last word. Encourage me, and help me to stand firm in your truth.

PG

Facing reality

After this I looked, and the temple of the tent of witness in heaven was opened, and out of the temple came the seven angels with the seven plagues, robed in pure bright linen, with golden sashes across their chests. Then one of the four living creatures gave the seven angels seven golden bowls full of the wrath of God, who lives for ever and ever; and the temple was filled with smoke from the glory of God and from his power, and no one could enter the temple until the seven plagues of the seven angels were ended.

Judgment is like turning on the headlights to reveal the landscape of our lives. God does not wish to punish us in a vindictive way, but because judgment and redemption belong together, he knows that we must face both our strengths and weaknesses realistically. Only then will we be ready to confront those areas of life in which we need to grow and be made whole.

Yesterday's reading forms the introduction to the vision of the seven plagues caused by the seven bowls of God's wrath. Deliberately intended to encourage Christians in an age of persecution, it focused on the heavenly music celebrating the victory of the Lamb. Now John challenges them to combat the subtle forces of evil, both in themselves and the world.

The tablets of the Ten Commandments embodied the holy will of God. During the wilderness wanderings of the exodus, they were kept in the tent of witness. Numbers 9:15 tells us that, from the day the tent was erected, a pillar of cloud by day and of fire by night rested on it. These were signs of the presence and holiness of God.

Now John shares his vision of the tent in heaven being opened so that the angels can step out to fulfil God's purpose. Dressed in dazzling robes of royal dignity and holiness, they radiate the light in which God dwells. They carry seven bowls containing his wrath, warning us of the punishment we deserve. All must face judgment, but, beyond it, for believers, there is the promise of a new heaven and a new Earth.

Reflection

'Indeed, God did not send the Son into the world to condemn the world, but in order that the world might be saved through him'
(John 3:17).

PG

The bowls of wrath

Then I heard a loud voice from the temple telling the seven angels, 'Go and pour out on the earth the seven bowls of the wrath of God.' So the first angel went and poured his bowl on the earth, and a foul and painful sore came on those who had the mark of the beast and who worshipped its image. The second angel poured his bowl into the sea, and it became like the blood of a corpse, and every living thing in the sea died.

The vision of seven angels pouring plagues from bowls of wrath reflects Revelation 8—11, which warns of terror following the sounding of seven trumpets. As these warnings have gone unheeded, everything now intensifies. The trumpets warned of limited destruction, but the plagues poured from the bowls are total. As the opportunity for repentance has passed, those not sealed as followers of the Lamb are marked as worshippers of the Beast, so they must be destroyed.

Chapter 15 reminded us of Moses who, in the name of God, told Pharaoh to 'let my people go'. By refusing, Pharaoh brought ten plagues on Egypt. Similarly, the worshippers of the Beast have refused God's warnings and must now face the consequences. The first bowl reflects the Egyptian plague of boils (Exodus 9:8–12); the second and third remind us of the Nile turning into blood (Exodus 7:14–24). John seems to be gathering all the horrors of Egypt and the trumpets together so that, in one last terrible deluge of disaster, they can be hurled on an unbelieving world.

Although we should not take the descriptive details of the plagues too literally, we need to hear the warning of judgment to come. We were not made to live in hostility to God. If we refuse to 'obey the maker's instructions' and so violate God's principles for life, we must bear the consequences.

John's hearers would have had no doubt that God existed and would have seen his hand in some of the events they were experiencing. Still they hardened their hearts and went their own way. By refusing to repent, they did, in effect, ally themselves with God's enemies. Are we so different?

Prayer

Forgive my weakness, Lord. Teach me the way of repentance and help me to live in trust and obedience!

PG

Light and darkness

The fourth angel poured his bowl on the sun, and it was allowed to scorch people with fire; they were scorched by the fierce heat, but they cursed the name of God, who had authority over these plagues, and they did not repent and give him glory. The fifth angel poured his bowl on the throne of the beast, and its kingdom was plunged into darkness; people gnawed their tongues in agony, and cursed the God of heaven because of their pains and sores, and they did not repent of their deeds.

The word 'Revelation' comes from the Latin and Greek for 'unveiling'. John seeks to reveal God's truth—not by logical argument, but in a more visual way. As in the parables, understanding comes as the message is seen and felt. With dramatic force, he confronts us with a quick-fire series of visions, images, scenes and symbols. This is clearly seen in these two plagues.

The suffering of the Beast and his followers is sharply contrasted with the blessing experienced by the faithful followers of the Lamb. From the sun comes the intense heat of judgment, whereas the faithful are promised 'the sun will not strike them, nor any scorching heat; for the Lamb at the centre of the throne will be their shepherd, and he will guide them to springs of the water of life' (Revelation 7:16–17).

The fifth angel invades the power base of the Beast. Like the ninth plague of Egypt (Exodus 10:21–23) darkness falls on his throne and the whole human system is thrown into disarray. The Antichrist has invaded the entire structure of society and perverted it to his own ends. Now he faces the full horrors of judgment as the victory of God is made manifest. Just as the Hebrews were exempted from the plagues of Egypt and had light when Egypt was in darkness, so the faithful will walk in the light of Christ's truth.

There is no room for Christian complacency, though. We sometimes claim to follow Christ, but live practically as atheists. We selfishly rebel and then blame God when things go wrong. Our pride does not wish to admit our need to repent, change the direction of our lives and start living in God's way.

Prayer

Lord, help me to 'walk the talk' and practise what I preach.

PG

The Battle of Harmagedon

The sixth angel poured his bowl on the great river Euphrates, and its water was dried up in order to prepare the way for the kings from the east. And I saw three foul spirits like frogs coming from the mouth of the dragon, from the mouth of the beast, and from the mouth of the false prophet. These are demonic spirits, performing signs, who go abroad to the kings of the whole world, to assemble them for battle on the great day of God the Almighty.... And they assembled them at the place that in Hebrew is called Harmagedon.

In Pharaoh's Egypt, the plague of darkness is followed by death. Similarly, the darkness of the kingdom of the Beast leads to the death and devastation of battle. In effect, Satan is saying, 'If I can no longer pervert, I will destroy' and so he prepares a mammoth confrontation. God, on the other hand, permits the battle as a means of bringing judgment and justice.

Foul spirits emanating from the mouth of the dragon (Satan) and the Beast persuade barbarian kings and their armies from beyond the eastern border of the Roman empire to cross the dried-up bed of the River Euphrates. They will then join the kings of the whole world for a frenzy of mutual slaughter.

'Armageddon' or 'Harmagedon' (in the NRSV) is a Greek transliteration of the Hebrew 'Har-Megiddo', which, literally, means the Hill of Megiddo. Overlooking the crossing place of some of the most important routes of the ancient world, from Arabia to Europe and Africa to Asia, Megiddo also witnessed many of the most crucial battles of history. Appropriately, therefore, it has become a symbol of war. It stands supremely for the last resistance of anti-God forces prior to the coming of the kingdom of Christ.

John's vision looks towards the 'great day of God the Almighty'— the final conflict between Christ and the powers of darkness. Because the day of the Lord will come when we least expect it, like a thief in the night, Christians must be prepared for it. We must stand firm for Christ, knowing that beyond the conflict will be the joy of victory.

Prayer

Lord, help me to live each day as if it were the last, so that I am always ready to meet you.

PG

The final judgment

The seventh angel poured his bowl into the air, and a loud voice came out of the temple, from the throne, saying, 'It is done!' And there came flashes of lightning, rumblings, peals of thunder, and a violent earthquake, such as had not occurred since people were upon the earth, so violent was the earthquake. The great city was split into three parts, and the cities of the nations fell. God remembered great Babylon and gave her the wine-cup of the fury of his wrath.

The Song of Moses and of the Lamb began this series of readings with a celebration of the greatness of God and his victory over the Beast. Encouragement and hope come from knowing of this ultimate victory, but there will be no new heaven or Earth without the crisis of judgment.

Today we read of a loud voice coming 'from the temple and the throne'. With holiness and authority, God declares the good news that his wrath is over, the work of judgment is done and the new age has dawned. Nevertheless, the punishment experienced on Earth is horrific. Nature is at war with humanity. As the air is polluted, human life is attacked at source. The bowl produces an earthquake of unprecedented severity and a storm of cataclysmic proportions. We move from time to eternity as islands and mountains vanish and the civilizations and cities of our selfish pride collapse.

As will be clearly seen in chapter 17 tomorrow, particular judgment falls on Babylon, the great city. John sees Rome as the centre of oppressive control and persecution, so it is not surprising that he often speaks of it as 'Babylon', but that is not the whole story. As the place of exile, Babylon was seen as an alien city, a symbol of the whole satanic structure, and of everything that contradicted the values of the kingdom of God. She thought she could do as she liked with impunity, but is now confronted with sin and its consequences. She must face judgment and drink the cup of God's wrath to its dregs.

Reflection

Judge eternal, throned in splendour,
Lord of lords and King of kings,
With Thy living fire of judgment,
Purge this realm of bitter things.
Solace all its wide dominion, With
the healing of Thy wings.

Henry Scott Holland (1847–1918)
PG

Priorities in perspective

I saw a woman sitting on a scarlet beast that was full of blasphemous names, and it had seven heads and ten horns. The woman was clothed in purple and scarlet, and adorned with gold and jewels and pearls, holding in her hand a golden cup full of abominations and the impurities of her fornication; and on her forehead was written a name, a mystery: 'Babylon the great, mother of whores and of earth's abominations.' And I saw that the woman was drunk with the blood of the saints and the blood of the witnesses to Jesus.

With the seventh bowl, God's punishment is complete. Now John wants us to see the judgment of Babylon in more detail and realize how dangerous is the evil that she represents.

Babylon is seen as a prostitute wearing the clothes of earthly pomp and luxury. She is seated on a seven-headed monster—an incarnation of evil. This beast is scarlet, a colour much loved in Rome as it represented royalty and conquering power. That it is full of blasphemous names reminds us that the empire embraced a multitude of forms of idolatry, including emperor worship. Whereas the beast controls and represses, the woman seduces. Together they draw us away from God. If the devil cannot succeed with persecution, he will try seduction!

Only God deserves worship. He should be the focus of our lives, so anything that distracts us from following him is idolatry. All too easily we get our priorities wrong and are subtly tricked into giving ultimate value to what is not ultimate. Sex, power and wealth are as seductive as ever and we are easily deceived in such matters. John's furious opposition to the power of the Beast, therefore, is not a rejection of all human authority, nor a suspicion of the good things of creation. He is angered by the dishonesty of idolatry that dilutes the power of faith, undermines the truth of the gospel and distracts us from living in accordance with God's will and purpose. Although the imagery of Revelation may sound strange to modern ears, we certainly need to hear the relevant and timely message that it proclaims.

Reflection

'Don't let the world around you squeeze you into its own mould, but let God remould your minds from within' (Romans 12:2, J.B. Phillips).

PG

Plumbing the depths and finding reality

'Fallen, fallen is Babylon the great! It has become a dwelling-place of demons... a haunt of every foul and hateful beast. For all the nations have drunk of the wine of the wrath of her fornication, and the kings of the earth have committed fornication with her, and the merchants of the earth have grown rich from the power of her luxury.... Come out of her, my people, so that you do not take part in her sins, and so that you do not share in her plagues; for her sins are heaped high as heaven, and God has remembered her iniquities.

Towards the end of the communist era in Poland, a visiting British cleric was intrigued to see that, whereas in England congregations were declining, the Polish churches were full. He discussed this with a local priest who said, 'We live in an atheistic state that is hostile to the Church and all that it stands for. We know what the issues are, and we must stand firm. In the West, you face a far more difficult challenge. You have to oppose the allurements of a superficial lifestyle.'

Revelation 18 declares the total overthrow of the city that ruled the world. It celebrates the judgment of the old order, which had become subject to the powers of evil. It then proclaims a new order under the sway of the Prince of Peace, and does so in the style of the Old Testament prophets. In their 'doom songs', they warned of judgment to come and challenged God's people to cut their connection with sin and stand with him. Idolatry had polluted true worship. Power had corrupted the rulers and the commercial world had so profited from material greed that it had been corrupted by the worship of 'Mammon'.

The world is powerful and its message so attractive that we are easily distracted from what is really important. So bound up with 'things temporal' are we that we lose sight of 'things eternal'. Instead, we are called to be 'in' the world, but not 'of' it. We do not follow the crowd. We have a higher calling. We march to the tune of a different drummer!

Sunday prayer

Forgive my superficiality, Lord, and lead me to the depths. Help me to worship you both in prayer and my daily walk as a follower of you.

PG

Mark 14—16: love unknown

What can we say about the final chapters of Mark that hasn't already been said many times by others? These chapters are not the most detailed account of Jesus' death and resurrection (indeed Mark's resurrection account seems to stop in the middle and there are two disputed endings to the Gospel), but they are perhaps the most stark and powerful narrative of these events.

Actually, over half of Mark's Gospel is devoted first to predictions of, then to the events of, Jesus' death. That Jesus died and was raised, Mark seems to say, is of equal importance to the fact that he lived. In my opinion, it does not have greater importance, however. We need to study the actions and teachings of Jesus' life or else our own Christian teaching and lives will end up dangerously unbalanced. We would then be tempted to focus too much on what Jesus has done for us and not enough on what we are called to do for, and in imitation of, him. His death could nevertheless be described as the 'crowning glory' of his life and his whole 'cross-shaped' life points to and leads up to it.

One thing I've particularly noticed in studying these chapters is how cleverly Mark weaves together a number of different stories: the betrayals of Judas and Peter, the faithfulness of the women, the trials of Jesus, the various statements other people make about him and that he makes about himself. The result is a rich picture of who Jesus is—the suffering servant, the wounded saviour, the king who comes to his rule by sacrificing himself, the redeemer who conquers death by dying. It is also a rich picture of how we, his modern-day disciples, are meant to respond—we are called to 'take up our own cross', learning to live a life in which we 'die to self'.

These are stories that repay careful study, but ultimately call us to meditate on them rather than analyse them. They are meant to drive us not to doctrinal statements, but to worship and service. They almost need a response in poetry, not prose. So, I have chosen to link them, on most days, with snatches of one of my favourite Easter hymns: 'My song is love unknown' by Samuel Crossman. To my surprise, it dates back to the 17th century, yet still speaks powerfully to followers of Jesus today.

Veronica Zundel

MARK 14:1–8 (NRSV, ABRIDGED)

Love in a jar

It was two days before the Passover and the festival of Unleavened Bread.... While he [Jesus] was at Bethany in the house of Simon the leper, as he sat at the table, a woman came with an alabaster jar of very costly ointment of nard, and she broke open the jar and poured the ointment on his head. But some were there who said to one another in anger, 'Why was the ointment wasted in this way?...' But Jesus said, 'Let her alone; why do you trouble her?... She has done what she could; she has anointed my body beforehand for its burial.'

A few days ago I learned that my husband and I would be receiving a substantial legacy from his mother, who sadly died recently. Now we have to decide what we will do with it. Invest it for the highest return? Invest it more safely? Put in into a social invest-ment to benefit the poorest? We could spend some—but on what? A new car? A large donation to charity?

Our readings in Mark begin and end with women and perfumed oils. This woman's precious jar of perfume was probably her nest egg—maybe a wedding gift or bought with years of savings. What did it represent for her—inde-pendence from an abusive hus-band? Escape from the streets?

It all went out of the window when she chose to massage it into Jesus' scalp. What motivated her? Perhaps she was moved by the fact that Jesus, unlike other men, had treated her with respect. It was a gesture of frank, unashamed love.

I have some sympathy with those who thought that this gift would have been better turned into cash to give to the poor. It is always easy to decide what other people should do with their money. Imagine, though, the com-fort it gave Jesus, seeing a horrific death drawing closer and getting no understanding from his friends, to experience this fragrant touch.

What gesture can we make to bring a moment of gladness to Jesus? Perhaps, in our case, we should make a gift to the poor, for he has said what we do for them, is done for him (Matthew 25:37–40).

Reflection

'Love to the loveless shown, that they might lovely be'. Lord, teach us to show love to the loveless, as you did.

VZ

Time to feast

On the first day of Unleavened Bread, when the Passover lamb is sacrificed, his disciples said to him, 'Where do you want us to go and make the preparations for you to eat the Passover?' So he sent two of his disciples, saying to them, 'Go into the city, and a man carrying a jar of water will meet you; follow him, and wherever he enters, say to the owner of the house, "The Teacher asks, Where is my guest room where I may eat the Passover with my disciples?" He will show you a large room upstairs, furnished and ready. Make preparations for us there.'

Every year my church celebrates a Passover meal in Holy Week. As I write, our church worker is frantically running round asking people which date they can make, if they can host a meal and trying to arrange things so that no one is left out.

Passover is the high feast of the year for practising Jews, and getting it ready can be as hectic as Christmas is for Christians. Jesus made it easier for his disciples. I'm intrigued by the detail of 'a man carrying a jar of water': water carrying was, as it still is in most of the world, women's work. Even at this most traditional of festivals, Jesus breaks the conventions.

I wonder how it felt, knowing that this would be his last Passover? I remember a few years ago, going to the Greenbelt Christian Arts Festival, having been diagnosed with breast cancer two days before. Throughout the festival, I was aware that this might be my last Greenbelt. I made sure to talk at length with every friend I met: if this were to be my last festival, I was going to make sure it was a good one. It was.

There is significance, of course, in Jesus' death coming at the time of this particular festival. Passover was the great feast of the Israelites' liberation from Egypt, when they were protected by the blood of an unblemished lamb that they smeared on their doorposts (Exodus 12:21–23). I don't need to spell out the parallels.

Reflection

'I tell you, many will come from east and west and will eat with Abraham and Isaac and Jacob in the kingdom of heaven' (Matthew 8:11). How significant is eating together in your church life?

VZ

So near, so far away

When it was evening, he came with the twelve. And when they had taken their places and were eating, Jesus said, 'Truly I tell you, one of you will betray me, one who is eating with me.' They began to be distressed and to say to him one after another, 'Surely, not I?' He said to them, 'It is one of the twelve, one who is dipping bread into the bowl with me. For the Son of Man goes as it is written of him, but woe to that one by whom the Son of Man is betrayed! It would have been better for that one not to have been born.'

My mother has been reading the autobiography of a contemporary of hers at medical school in 1930s' Vienna. This woman, from a wealthy American Methodist background, was not a Christian herself, yet risked her life over and over to save Jews from extermination.

I also know that there were churches and individuals who bore the name of Christ yet did nothing to help those facing imprisonment and death—indeed, some even approved of Hitler's policies. The militias who massacred Palestinians in the refugee camps of Lebanon in 1982 also bore the name 'Christian'. Wherever the Church exists, there will be some who 'belong' to it, yet have not absorbed Jesus' values.

The story of Judas is a terrifying one. It tells us that it is possible to hear Jesus' words day after day, be in Jesus' presence and that of his friends, eat bread and wine with Jesus and yet still betray him. As Jesus said, 'Not everyone who says to me, "Lord, Lord" will enter the kingdom…' (Matthew 7: 21).

Paul suggests in 1 Corinthians, in the context of discussing Communion, that 'all who eat and drink without discerning the body, eat and drink judgment against themselves' (11:29). I believe that this is about discerning that those with whom you worship are the body of Christ (1 Corinthians 12:12–14). If we do not recognize that what we do to others, we are doing to Christ, then our participation in worship is meaningless.

Yet, Jesus invited Judas to the feast nevertheless. Grace reached out to him until the end.

Prayer

'Never was love, dear King, never was grief like thine.'

VZ

A matter of death—and life

While they were eating, he took a loaf of bread, and after blessing it he broke it, gave it to them, and said, 'Take; this is my body.' Then he took a cup, and after giving thanks he gave it to them, and all of them drank from it. He said to them, 'This is my blood of the covenant, which is poured out for many. Truly I tell you, I will never again drink of the fruit of the vine until that day when I drink it new in the kingdom of God.'

'I have often walked down this street before/But the pavement always stayed beneath my feet before': so sings the young lover in the musical *My Fair Lady*. Somehow, love can totally transform something that, until now, was just routine.

Passover was very familiar for Jesus' Jewish disciples and maybe for them there was a sense of 'here we are again' about it. Jesus suddenly breaks out of the accepted liturgy, though, and declares, 'This is all about me.' It must have been as shocking as his first sermon in Nazareth, when he made the same declaration about the day's reading from Isaiah (Luke 4:21).

Not only is he radically rewriting the meaning of the Passover meal, but he is asking these Jews to do something that would be uterly repugnant to them—to think of this wine as blood *and still drink it*. Consuming blood had been forbidden since the time of Noah (Genesis 9:4) and it was (and still is) a distinctive mark of being Jewish. Was this a factor that decided Judas to turn against Jesus?

Think about what this new symbolism means. The bread and wine we eat and drink at Communion enter right inside us and are absorbed into our very cells. What a powerful image of Jesus of living in us, becoming part of our very physical being!

It is also, of course, an image of his death. Paul said that by eating the bread and drinking the cup we 'proclaim the Lord's death, until he comes' (1 Corinthians 11:26). We also reaffirm our willingness to share in that death, which we first committed ourselves to in the waters of baptism (Romans 6:3).

Reflection

'Oh who am I, that for my sake my Lord should take frail flesh and die?'

VZ

In deep distress

They went to a place called Gethsemane; and he said to his disciples, 'Sit here while I pray.' He took with him Peter and James and John, and began to be distressed and agitated. And he said to them, 'I am deeply grieved, even to death; remain here, and keep awake.' And going a little farther, he threw himself on the ground and prayed that, if it were possible, the hour might pass from him. He said, 'Abba, Father, for you all things are possible; remove this cup from me; yet, not what I want, but what you want.' He came and found them sleeping; and he said to Peter, 'Simon, are you asleep? Could you not keep awake one hour?'

'Yet cheerful he to suffering goes'. This is the point at which I disagree strongly with my chosen hymn! Jesus did not 'go cheerfully' to suffering; nor would he have agreed with that popular meditation that claims 'Death is nothing at all'. He knew that death was 'the last enemy' (1 Corinthians 15:26), the 'shroud that is cast over all peoples' (Isaiah 25:7). He is filled with horror at facing it, as he was filled with horror about the death of Lazarus (John 11:33–35).

I'm not sure about the second part of the phrase from the hymn either—'that he his foes from thence might free'. Jesus died to save us from futility and destruction, but did he die to free us from all suffering? If he did, it hasn't worked very well! Christians still suffer, whether at the hands of those who do evil or simply from the circumstances of life.

Yes, you may answer, but the Bible tells us 'whenever you face trials of any kind, consider it nothing but joy' (James 1:2). There is a very funny note on this by Adrian Plass, republished in his book *When You Walk* (BRF, 1997) where he dramatizes 'a typical day in the Plass household'. The car breaks down, all sorts of other things go wrong, but Adrian and Bridget merely exclaim 'Oh what joy!' This is not how it is or how it is meant to be. God wants us to say honestly how we feel when we're suffering. Jesus did.

Prayer

'Save me, O God, for the waters have come up to my neck' (Psalm 69:1).

VZ

MARK 14:43–50 (NRSV, ABRIDGED)

Two betrayals

Immediately, while he was still speaking, Judas, one of the twelve, arrived; and with him there was a crowd with swords and clubs, from the chief priests, the scribes, and the elders. Now the betrayer had given them a sign, saying, 'The one I will kiss is the man; arrest him and lead him away under guard.' So when he came, he went up to him at once and said, 'Rabbi!' and kissed him. Then they laid hands on him and arrested him. But one of those who stood near drew his sword and struck the slave of the high priest, cutting off his ear.... All of them deserted him and fled.

Now here's a difficult question: who betrayed Jesus more—Judas or Peter? Judas, as far as we know, never cried out with Peter, 'Even though I must die with you, I will not deny you' (14:31). He had already left to meet the authorities by then. Peter, however, makes extravagant claims of loyalty. Yet the moment the armed crowd arrives, he completely forgets his promise to die along with Jesus and instead draws his sword (John names the sword-wielder as Peter in John 18:10). Is this not Peter's first betrayal—a betrayal of the one who said that 'all who take the sword will perish by the sword' (Matthew 26:52)? Yes, I know Jesus earlier told the disciples that they needed to buy swords (Luke 22:35–38), but I believe that was just an 'acted sign' of approaching danger. He never told them to use them.

A growing number of Christians believe that whenever we take up the sword—or gun or cluster bomb or nuclear armoury—we are betraying Jesus, who came as the Prince of Peace and taught us to 'love your enemies' (Luke 6:35) and whose apostles Paul and Peter both told their followers, 'Do not repay anyone evil for evil' (Romans 12:17, 1 Peter 3:9).

This is a hard lesson, on a personal let alone a national level. After a New Year service, a very unstable fellow church member gratuitously insulted me out of the blue. I confess I broke all resolutions and responded with the bluest of language—thank God I didn't have a sword!

Reflection

'But men made strange, and none the longed-for Christ would know'.

VZ

Silence in court

Now the chief priests and the whole council were looking for testimony against Jesus to put him to death; but they found none. For many gave false testimony against him, and their testimony did not agree. Some stood up and gave false testimony against him, saying, 'We heard him say, "I will destroy this temple that is made with hands, and in three days I will build another, not made with hands."'... Then the high priest stood up before them and asked Jesus, 'Have you no answer? What is it that they testify against you?' But he was silent and did not answer.

'So she said to me…', 'No, that's not what I said…' Have you ever had a conflict where everything hinges on what was actually said? It's almost impossible to disentangle, unless you tape every conversation. The best option is to bring people together with a mediator and expose the underlying feelings beneath the 'he said', 'she said' game so that they can be resolved.

In the conflict between Jesus and the religious authorities, however, the minds of the prosecutors were made up. They were not searching for truth, but for an appropriate capital charge that they could use to get rid of this troublemaker.

Ironically, the testimony of the false witnesses is partly true. Jesus did indeed predict an end to the temple system and did build 'a temple not made with hands'—we, his followers, are it. True or not, however, he says nothing in his defence: 'he did not open his mouth; like a lamb that is led to the slaughter' (Isaiah 53:7). Not, that is, until the high priest asks directly 'Are you the Messiah?' when he answers, 'I am' (14:61–62). Unlike Peter, he has abandoned his instinct for self-preservation—he is here to preserve others.

Many followers of Jesus around the world still face rigged trials and horrible deaths, whether for their desire to worship or standing up for justice and peace. Could it happen to us? If it did, I hope we would value truth above our own safety and rely on the Holy Spirit to give us the words we would need (Luke 21:12–15).

Sunday reflection

'Sometimes they strew his way, And his sweet praises sing; Resounding all the day Hosannas to the King'. How can you make your Palm Sunday praises more than lip-service?

VZ

MARK 14:66–72 (NRSV, ABRIDGED)

Denial and despair

While Peter was below in the courtyard, one of the servant-girls of the high priest came by. When she saw Peter warming himself, she stared at him and said, 'You also were with Jesus, the man from Nazareth.' But he denied it, saying, 'I do not know or understand what you are talking about.' … Then the cock crowed… Then after a little while the bystanders again said to Peter, 'Certainly you are one of them; for you are a Galilean.' But he began to curse, and he swore an oath, 'I do not know this man you are talking about.' At that moment the cock crowed for the second time. Then Peter remembered that Jesus had said to him, 'Before the cock crows twice, you will deny me three times.' And he broke down and wept.

The other day a mum from my son's school exclaimed, 'I hate religion for all the trouble it causes!' Then she suddenly remembered I was a Christian and apologized. I tried to point out that not all religious people cause wars, but as everyone talks at once in that particular parents' group, I didn't get much chance!

It might have been easier if I hadn't mentioned early on that I was a Christian, but it wasn't a matter of life and death, as it was for Peter. I can sympathize with his desire to protect himself.

As I suggested earlier, both Judas and Peter betrayed Jesus, so what's the difference? Perhaps it is that Peter stayed around long enough to experience Jesus' forgiveness (John 21:15). Judas gave in to despair (Matthew 27:3–5). He felt remorse, but he didn't really repent in the sense of turning back to God. Thus 'Judas' has become a term of abuse, while Peter became the first leader of the Church.

Could Judas have been forgiven? I don't know. I only know that Peter was. We all commit our small or larger betrayals of Jesus in what we say or how we live. Our only hope is to follow Peter's example and come, with all our tears of regret, to the God who, in Christ, has taken our sins on himself.

Reflection

'But O, my Friend, my Friend indeed, who at my need his life did spend.' Thank God today for the forgiveness you have through Jesus.

VZ

MARK 15:1, 6–13 (NRSV)

The other prisoner

As soon as it was morning, the chief priests held a consultation with the elders and scribes and the whole council. They bound Jesus, led him away, and handed him over to Pilate.... Now at the festival he used to release a prisoner for them, anyone for whom they asked. Now a man called Barabbas was in prison with the rebels who had committed murder during the insurrection. So the crowd came and began to ask Pilate to do for them according to his custom. Then he answered them, 'Do you want me to release for you the King of the Jews?'... But the chief priests stirred up the crowd to have him release Barabbas for them instead. Pilate spoke to them again, 'Then what do you wish me to do with the man you call the King of the Jews?' They shouted back, 'Crucify him!'

What would we call Barabbas if he were alive today? I suspect that, to his fellow Jews, he would be a freedom fighter. To the Roman authorities, he would be a terrorist. Depending on which group we identify with, we see him either as a political hero or a dangerous murderer.

His part in this story is full of irony: 'A murderer they save, the Prince of Life they slay'. Barabbas' name means, literally, 'father's son'. Barabbas is a mirror image of Jesus, who accepts an unjust death, while he inflicts death and goes free. Could he also stand for all of us—the 'archetypal sinner', set free by Jesus' death?

I don't know how the cross 'works'. The Bible itself has a number of theories, but all I know is that I see there a God who, rather than inflict violence, is willing to have it inflicted on him. I see a God who mysteriously identifies with our weakness and sin so that, in exchange, we are identified with God's goodness. I also see an example for us to follow that, as his students (which is what 'disciples' means), we, too, are meant to be ready to die rather than kill, love rather than to hate.

Reflection

'Then "Crucify!" is all their breath, and for his death they thirst and cry.' When we do nothing about the death of the innocent, how different are we from that crowd?

VZ

The torture victim

Then the soldiers led him into the courtyard of the palace (that is, the governor's headquarters); and they called together the whole cohort. And they clothed him in a purple cloak; and after twisting some thorns into a crown, they put it on him. And they began saluting him, 'Hail, King of the Jews!' They struck his head with a reed, spat upon him, and knelt down in homage to him. After mocking him, they stripped him of the purple cloak and put his own clothes on him. Then they led him out to crucify him.

Until recently, we might have dismissed this ill-treatment of a prisoner as something done by barbaric people, something that would never happen in our 'civilized' nation. After hearing of prisoner abuse committed by 'the good side' in the Iraq war, however, we cannot be too complacent. The Romans also thought of themselves as 'civilized'. The brutality of these soldiers may not be far beneath the skin of any of us. I suspect that, in a group of people trained to kill, there will inevitably be some for whom their training brings out an innate cruelty. That's one of the reasons for my personal belief that we shouldn't instruct people in such ways.

There are deeper meanings, however, to the abuse that these Roman soldiers inflict. First, another of Mark's ironies. The title they mockingly give Jesus—'King of the Jews'—is, in fact, just what Mark wants to tell us he is. Second, there is a sense in which Jesus here stands for every man, woman and child who suffers at the hands of the cynical and uncaring.

Jacob Epstein's controversial statue 'Ecce Homo' (Latin for 'Behold the man') stands in the ruined cathedral in Coventry where I grew up. It portrays Jesus, crowned with thorns and bound at the wrists, in the style of a prehistoric carving. I think he is saying that Jesus in his suffering is 'Everyman', taking on himself the whole history of the sufferings and sin of humankind. I think he's got it right.

By our indifference, ignorance or greed, we are all capable of inflicting torture on Jesus in the person of those who suffer from the barbarity of war or the degradation of hunger and disease.

Prayer

Lord, make me an instrument of your peace, not an instrument of your torture.

VZ

MARK 15:25–32 (NRSV, ABRIDGED)

The final test

It was nine o'clock in the morning when they crucified him. The inscription of the charge against him read, 'The King of the Jews.'… Those who passed by derided him, shaking their heads and saying, 'Aha! You who would destroy the temple and build it in three days, save yourself, and come down from the cross!' In the same way the chief priests, along with the scribes, were also mocking him among themselves and saying, 'He saved others; he cannot save himself. Let the Messiah, the King of Israel, come down from the cross now, so that we may see and believe.' Those who were crucified with him also taunted him.

'If you are the son of God…'. Mark doesn't record Jesus' testing in the desert in detail, but I can't help thinking of Luke's account when I read this scene. Anyone worthy of the title written over the cross, the onlookers seem to be saying, would now be ripping the nails out like the Incredible Hulk ripping his shirt. Is that the kind of saviour we sometimes secretly want? A superhero, who will fix every world problem with a wave of the hand?

This 'weak' image of God is no more popular today. 'If the story of Jesus is true,' many voices say, 'why isn't the world a better place? Why doesn't God sort everything out?' Some Christians respond by pretending God does, that if you follow Jesus, you will never be in suffering or want.

In fact, the very opposite is true. 'A disciple is not above the teacher, nor a slave above the master' (Matthew 10:24). If Jesus brings salvation by way of non-violent, suffering love, we should not expect to walk in his footsteps and find things to be any other way. God still chooses to work through the weak, the vulnerable, the oppressed and the damaged and that is where we will most find God.

So, once again, the mockers are telling the truth: it is only by refusing to save himself, that Jesus can save others. Likewise for us: 'Those who find their life will lose it, and those who lose their life for my sake will find it' (Matthew 10:39).

Reflection

'Why, what hath my Lord done? What makes this rage and spite? He made the lame to run, he gave the blind their sight.'

VZ

'Tis mystery all

When it was noon, darkness came over the whole land until three in the afternoon. At three o'clock Jesus cried out with a loud voice, 'Eloi, Eloi, lema sabachthani?' which means, 'My God, my God, why have you forsaken me?' When some of the bystanders heard it, they said, 'Listen, he is calling for Elijah.' And someone ran, filled a sponge with sour wine, put it on a stick, and gave it to him to drink, saying, 'Wait, let us see whether Elijah will come to take him down.' Then Jesus gave a loud cry and breathed his last. And the curtain of the temple was torn in two, from top to bottom. Now when the centurion, who stood facing him, saw that in this way he breathed his last, he said, 'Truly this man was God's Son!'

The late medieval painter Grünewald painted the crucified Christ for a hospital altarpiece as horribly twisted and covered in wounds. The 20th-century surrealist Dali portrayed him hung in the sky, unwounded, held to the cross not by nails but by love. Bach set Jesus' Passion to heartrending music. Throughout Christian history, artists, musicians, writers have all offered their own interpretations of these dramatic, world-changing events.

Our reading today also offers different interpretations. There is Jesus' own experience—the agony of feeling abandoned by his Father, his closest companion. There is the interpretation of the bystanders, who try to fit him into their own scheme of salvation and find him lacking. Then there is the most surprising of all—the centurion's reaction. How did this career soldier feel when he had that sudden insight? Overwhelmed with guilt? Confused as to why God would let this man die? Wondering how he could live with this killing and this knowledge?

The cross is taught, and perceived, in many different ways. For some, it may induce guilt and fear: 'Look what we have done to God.' For others, it is the sign of total forgiveness: 'Look what God has done for us'. Some see it as God taking the punishment for our sin; others as God entering into our suffering. Whatever your response, once you really see it—with insight into who Jesus was and is—it is impossible to ignore.

Reflection

In his death is our birth.

VZ

Small mercies

There were also women looking on from a distance.... These used to follow him and provided for him when he was in Galilee.... When evening had come, and since it was the day of Preparation, that is, the day before the sabbath, Joseph of Arimathea, a respected member of the council, who was also himself waiting expectantly for the kingdom of God, went boldly to Pilate and asked for the body of Jesus.... Then Joseph bought a linen cloth, and taking down the body, wrapped it in the linen cloth, and laid it in a tomb that had been hewn out of the rock. He then rolled a stone against the door of the tomb. Mary Magdalene and Mary the mother of Joses saw where the body was laid.

Sometimes I think about how much need there is in the world and how little I, even with others, can do to change it and I feel useless as a servant of God's kingdom. Then, this passage is reassuring.

First, the women reappear and we learn that they, unlike the other disciples, have never deserted Jesus. They can do nothing to prevent his death, but still they stand faithfully watching. That's something I can do: not give up on believing in him, loving him and serving him. In fact, the women, by their mere presence, become vital witnesses that Jesus has really died and, later, that he has risen. This, despite a woman's testimony being invalid in law at that time— evidently God thought it enough!

Then there is Joseph—the first we have heard of this highly placed, but secret, believer. If Peter wanted to save his own skin by denying Jesus, Joseph had far more to lose. Yet he took the risk of going public, to do the only thing he could now for Jesus: to bury him.

I too, can only do what is in my power. I believe God graciously accepts it. More than this, I believe I will be amazed—as were Joseph, the women and the other disciples—by what God can do with the little I offer. I'm sure Joseph didn't expect to get his family tomb back so soon!

Reflection

'What may I say? Heaven was his home, but mine the tomb wherein he lay.'

VZ

He is risen

When the sabbath was over, Mary Magdalene, and Mary the mother of James, and Salome bought spices, so that they might go and anoint him. And very early on the first day of the week, when the sun had risen, they went to the tomb. They had been saying to one another, 'Who will roll away the stone for us from the entrance to the tomb?' When they looked up, they saw that the stone, which was very large, had already been rolled back. As they entered the tomb, they saw a young man, dressed in a white robe, sitting on the right side; and they were alarmed. But he said to them, 'Do not be alarmed; you are looking for Jesus of Nazareth, who was crucified. He has been raised; he is not here….'

The older I get, the more convinced I am that without the resurrection there is no hope for any of us. Paul (I'm glad to say) came to the same conclusion: 'If for this life only we have hoped in Christ, we are of all people most to be pitied' (1 Corinthians 15:19).

Notice that Paul doesn't say: 'There is no hope except in the next life.' Rather, there is no hope in this life, unless there is something from outside it that redeems it. Human suffering is not the last word. However, it requires the testimony of those women—the ones who are still, in today's reading, doing what little they can for the Jesus they still assume to be dead—to change the picture from the darkness of Good Friday to the light of Easter Sunday.

It still requires the testimony—and actions—of women and men who have met the risen Jesus to change the world in which we live. We still need to proclaim, in word and deed, 'He has been raised.' Sometimes we will have to proclaim that against all the apparent evidence and in spite of, not because, of our circumstances and feelings. Our testimony, however, is slightly different from that of the angel to the women: 'He has been raised; *he is here*.' That is the divine reversal, the event that turns tragedy into joy; our hope for this life and the next.

Sunday praise

'Here might I stay and sing no story so divine.'

VZ

Malachi

I gather that the Hebrew word 'malachi' means 'messenger', but we have no way of definitely knowing if Malachi is the name of the prophet who delivered these messages. There is no record of anyone else using this name. Whatever the case, it doesn't really matter. The words of this prophet, whatever his name was, are very powerful ones and a weighty percentage of what he has to say is about uncommitted worship. At the time of writing, the temple had been rebuilt for quite a long time and it seems that the priests had become very half-hearted about their duties. In particular, they had stopped bringing the best of their animals for sacrifice, preferring instead to use sick or deformed creatures that would not be missed.

In addition, Jewish men were abandoning and divorcing the wives of their youth, taking up instead with women of exotic foreign faiths—something that had always enraged God. The whole nation at this time seems to have lost its faith and its nerve, moving away from God because it appeared, on the face of it, that the wicked were prospering more than the righteous.

Through his prophet, God calls the priests and the people to repentance, reminding them of what he has done for them in the past and warning them of the consequences if they fail to get their act together. He calls for a tenth of all that they produce to be brought to him and promises that, in return, the floodgates of his blessing will be thrown open. He will protect their crops and make sure that their harvests are greater than the capacity of storehouses that are supposed to contain them.

The book of Malachi is not exactly a barrel of laughs, but it does have some very relevant and important things to say to the Church of the 21st century. We are no longer obliged to sort through our flocks to select an appropriate goat for sacrifice, but we still have to decide the quality of our service to God—whether it is in terms of money, time, morality, care for others or general commitment. More than anything else, the book of Malachi is a cry from the heart of God for an adjustment of priorities. Who or what is the most important thing in our lives? If the honest answer to that question is not God, what, if anything, do we plan to do about it?

Adrian Plass

MALACHI 1:1–5 (NIV)

Looking back

An oracle: The word of the Lord to Israel through Malachi. 'I have loved you,' says the Lord. 'But you ask, "How have you loved us?" Was not Esau Jacob's brother?' the Lord says. 'Yet I have loved Jacob, but Esau I have hated, and I have turned his mountains into a wasteland and left his inheritance to the desert jackals.' Edom may say, 'Though we have been crushed, we will rebuild the ruins.' But this is what the Lord Almighty says: 'They may build, but I will demolish. They will be called the Wicked Land, a people always under the wrath of the Lord. You will see it with your own eyes and say, "Great is the Lord—even beyond the borders of Israel!"'

My wife and I had a dip in spirits recently. Negative bombshells landed one after another. We felt battered and bruised and slightly resentful towards God, who, as the one with power, we thought might have done something about it. We human beings are so fickle. When we get into this frame of mind, everything tends to go out the window. Out goes the furniture of our faith, dumped unceremoniously so that we can more easily relish the misery of abandonment. For a while, a cold, Godless space is more attractive than any sense of his presence. Foolish thinking, of course. As far as I am concerned, sanity is only starting to return as I look at the things that God has already done in my life, things that vastly outshine this present moment of darkness.

That is what God is saying to his people here when they grumpily ask how he has loved them. 'Remember Edom,' he tells them through Malachi. 'That nation caused trouble when you made your desert journey from Egypt to Canaan and recently they joined in the looting when Jerusalem and Judah were overthrown. Now Edom has been finally defeated and destroyed and will never be rebuilt. Israel, on the other hand, has been amazingly restored, brought back from exile and encouraged to rebuild the temple. What other evidence do you need of my love?' Well, exactly.

Prayer

Father, forgive us when we forget the love you have shown us in the past. Help us not to be childish. Thank you for watching over us.

AP

Second best

'A son honours his father, and a servant his master. If I am a father, where is the honour due me? If I am a master, where is the respect due me?' says the Lord Almighty. 'It is you, O priests, who show contempt for my name. But you ask, "How have we shown contempt for your name?" You place defiled food on my altar. But you ask, "How have we defiled you?" By saying that the Lord's table is contemptible. When you bring blind animals for sacrifice, is that not wrong? When you sacrifice crippled or diseased animals, is that not wrong? Try offering them to your governor! Would he be pleased with you? Would he accept you?' says the Lord Almighty.

This extract from Malachi has been on my mind for ages. There is a weight of hurt and outrage in these complaints from God that profoundly moves my spirit. These priests (we are all priests now, so it could be us) have stopped believing that God deserves the very best. When a beast is needed for sacrifice, they choose a goat that might have died anyway or a lamb so deformed that it has little worldly value.

Now, we human beings are rather simple creatures. When we stop valuing something, we no longer want to pay for it. On a level where it really matters, these priests had stopped believing that God had any real relevance to their lives. Why waste good, healthy, valuable animals on someone who offered them nothing in return?

Nowadays, I suppose the problem boils down to lack of belief.

People might wish that they did believe wholeheartedly, but are wary of investing very much time, money, attention or involvement in a God or a community that may have no ultimate value for them.

Let us be quite clear. God is not interested in the jumble sale rubbish of our lives, the stuff that, because we have no use for it anyway, we don't mind giving away. It shows a lack of respect and love. It hurts and angers him. We don't want that, do we?

Prayer

Father, some of us have tried to fob you off with cheap and tawdry offerings. Forgive us. We resolve to offer you the very best of our time, attention and material resources as a token of love and respect.

AP

MALACHI 1:9–13 (NIV)

Useless fires

'Now implore God to be gracious to us. With such offerings from your hands, will he accept you?'—says the Lord Almighty. 'Oh, that one of you would shut the temple doors, so that you would not light useless fires on my altar! I am not pleased with you,' says the Lord Almighty, 'and I will accept no offering from your hands. My name will be great among the nations, from the rising to the setting of the sun. In every place incense and pure offerings will be brought to my name, because my name will be great among the nations,' says the Lord Almighty. 'But you profane it by saying of the Lord's table, "It is defiled," and of its food "It is contemptible." And you say, "What a burden!" and you sniff at it contemptuously,' says the Lord Almighty.

How many 'useless fires' are lit in churches around the world every Sunday? These fires crackle and pop and are filled with colour, but offer no genuine heat to the chilled body of Christ. This can happen for many reasons. I remember, for instance, speaking at a church where the worship time preceding my talk was about as perfect in musical terms as it could be. The music ebbed and flowed with flawless precision, while the singers sang so skilfully and in such perfect harmony that it was a joy to listen to, and yet…

What is the element missing from otherwise excellent church music when it simply does not work? That was my feeling as I sat and listened to the instrumentalists and the vocalists: something essential was absent from all those carefully organized sounds. Spiritual confidence, perhaps? A detachment from the roots of worship? A lack of heart? I found out later. Days earlier the minister of the church had admitted to long-term adultery with a member of his congregation and the technical near perfection of the music was a desperate attempt to paper over deep cracks that had opened in that church community. The worship session I witnessed never reached heaven and it never left the ground. Facts and feelings need to be faced. Tears and silence would have been more useful. It was a useless fire and it warmed nobody.

Prayer

Father, grant that the fires we light for you will be useful ones.

AP

Hedging their bets

'When you bring injured, crippled or diseased animals and offer them as sacrifices, should I accept them from your hands?' says the Lord. 'Cursed is the cheat who has an acceptable male in his flock and vows to give it, but then sacrifices a blemished animal to the Lord. For I am a great king,' says the Lord Almighty, 'and my name is to be feared among the nations. And now this admonition is for you, O priests. If you do not listen, and if you do not set your heart to honour my name,' says the Lord Almighty, 'I will send a curse upon you, and I will curse your blessings. Yes, I have already cursed them, because you have not set your heart to honour me.'

A man wrote to me saying that he found it difficult to understand the story of Ananias and Sapphira. This unfortunate couple appear in Acts chapter 5. They donated half the proceeds from the sale of a field to a church's funds, claiming that they had given the full amount—a very silly move given that they were dealing with Peter. He instantly detected their lie. The husband and wife both dropped dead at his feet, causing the whole church (not surprisingly!) to be seized with fear. My correspondent thought that this was a startlingly harsh response to a 'fib'. The couple had, after all, given half their money to the church, so why was God so very tough on them?

I'm afraid I had no satisfactory answer to that question at the time, but thinking about it now, perhaps their offence was greater than it might appear at first sight.

Ananias and Sapphira were under no pressure to give all, or indeed any, of their money to their church and the fact that they lied to the Holy Spirit indicates three things that also apply to the 'cheat' in this passage, who brought a manky old goat along to be sacrificed instead of the decent one that he had promised. First, they did not actually believe in the power of God to see into the hearts of men and women and, second, they were anxious to hedge their bets in case the whole thing turned out to be true. Third, they had no respect.

We cannot play these silly games with God. They make him extremely angry.

A thought

A cursed blessing is worse than no blessing at all.

AP

MALACHI 2:3–6 (NIV)

A graphic threat

'Because of you I will rebuke your descendants; I will spread on your faces the offal from your festival sacrifices, and you will be carried off with it. And you will know that I have sent you this admonition so that my covenant with Levi may continue,' says the Lord Almighty. 'My covenant was with him, a covenant of life and peace, and I gave them to him; this called for reverence and he revered me and stood in awe of my name. True instruction was in his mouth and nothing false was found on his lips. He walked with me in peace and uprightness, and turned many from sin.'

The descendants of Jacob's son Levi were set aside to be a tribe of priests and Levi himself was a shining example for those who were to follow. He was deeply reverent towards God and careful and faithful in his teaching of God's truth. His own way of life was the best example of all. Now God is calling for these pathetic priests of his to remember the relationship that existed between himself and Levi and mend their ways accordingly.

The threat that is issued against them if they fail to respond is graphic, to say the least. I can't help playing with the idea that, let us say, Anglican ordinands, might be warned in advance of taking up their posts that chronic disobedience and failure would be met with a divinely administered faceful of dung (so the NRSV has it). That should sort out the possibles from the probables, don't you think?

Bizarre though that specific concept might appear to us, it vividly illustrates the rage of God against those who were neglecting their sacred responsibility. As well as rejecting life and peace for themselves, they were failing those who might have turned away from sin and towards God if a good example and true instruction had been available to them.

In this age we say a lot about the love of God. We should—his love is behind every good thing that has ever happened to us. At the same time, though, let us not forget his anger. We are priests with a solemn responsibility for protecting his image. We are bound to let him down sometimes, but let's pray that it won't happen too often.

Prayer

Lord, don't let it happen too often.

AP

Causing others to stumble

'For the lips of a priest ought to preserve knowledge and from his mouth men should seek instruction—because he is the messenger of the Lord Almighty. But you have turned from the way and by your teaching have caused many to stumble; you have violated the covenant with Levi,' says the Lord Almighty. 'So I have caused you to be despised and humiliated before all the people, because you have not followed my ways but have shown partiality in matters of the law.'

'By your teaching you have caused many to stumble,' says God. After reading these words, I sat and stared out of my study window, reflecting on the fact that I spend a lot of time telling people what I think about God and the Bible and the Christian faith. Has my incessant bleating caused anyone to stumble in the past? Would I be aware if it had? I honestly cannot answer these questions, but I know that sometimes I have continued with what one might loosely term 'ministry' at moments when my life was not in order and my ears were closed to the voice of the Spirit. Now that I think about it, I also recall the odd conversation where I have got out of my depth intellectually or emotionally and become a religious bully in order to protect myself from the possibility of sounding like an idiot. How might a performance of that kind have affected those who were listening from the side, as it

were? Impossible to be sure, of course, but I think I might make an even greater effort in future to keep my mouth shut when I know that my three penn'orth is essentially self-serving.

I suppose one important aspect of this situation is that most of the Christian speakers and writers I know do really care about the consequences of their words and are not expecting to be despised and humiliated by God because of an occasional slip-up. The heart of that confidence is important. My experience is that, having known and received the love of God as a Father, the fear of hurting him is far more powerful than the threat of punishment. I shall ask him to protect me from the possibility of letting anyone else down and thereby grieving his heart.

Prayer
Guard my lips, Lord.

AP

Filthy and detestable

Have we not all one Father? Did not one God create us? Why do we profane the covenant of our fathers by breaking faith with one another? Judah has broken faith. A detestable thing has been committed in Israel and in Jerusalem: Judah has desecrated the sanctuary the Lord loves by the daughter of a foreign god. As for the man who does this, whoever he may be, may the Lord cut him off from the tents of Jacob—even though he brings offerings to the Lord Almighty.

In one sense I take Genesis to Malachi with a pillar—sorry, I mean a pinch—of salt. We must use care and discrimination in applying parts of the Old Testament directly to this age. (The Anglican dung-smearing idea is one example, stoning your teenagers to death when they misbehave is another.) Everything should be viewed through the clearest revelation of God available to us—Jesus himself, who is described in Colossians chapter 1 as 'the image of the invisible God'. This is not the same as saying that the Old Testament is unimportant or irrelevant. On the contrary, it is crucial to our understanding of God's dealings with us past, present and future. We must not neglect it. Now, having said all that, there are themes in the Old Testament that are so repeatedly and passionately expressed that they have carry an immediate authenticity. This passage embodies one of them.

Our God is a jealous God. He has lavished love, guidance, discipline and redemption on the world he loves so much and is not about to share us with any other priority that has entered our lives, whether that is an actual foreign god or some more worldly pursuit or obsession that has stolen and occupied his rightful place in our hearts. For the one true God, our God, there is a disgusting filthiness, a detestable stench about the very notion that we, his children, might be drawn away to worship false gods or idols or windsurfing or sex or philosophies or alcohol or abstinence or religion or principles or anything else if it has become more important to us than him. He hates it and he will not put up with it in this or any other age.

Sunday prayer

Lord, you are Lord. We worship you.

AP

Repenting boldly

Another thing you do: You flood the Lord's altar with tears. You weep and wail because he no longer pays attention to your offerings or accepts them with pleasure from your hands. You ask, 'Why?' It is because the Lord is acting as the witness between you and the wife of your youth, because you have broken faith with her, though she is your partner, the wife of your marriage covenant. Has not the Lord made them one? In flesh and spirit they are his. And why one? Because he was seeking godly offspring. So guard yourself in your spirit, and do not break faith with the wife of your youth. 'I hate divorce,' says the Lord God of Israel, 'and I hate a man's covering himself with violence as well as with his garment,' says the Lord Almighty. So guard yourself in your spirit, and do not break faith.

I have heard quoted a letter from Martin Luther to a friend, urging him to sin boldly and repent boldly. Presumably Luther meant that, if you have sinned, you should be upfront about it and not make excuses.

'I'd had a bad day, you see…', 'You have to understand the context…', 'You have no idea what I'd been putting up with…'—I've used all those in the past, as well as a few others that I can't remember at the moment, and none of them transmute sin into anything other than what it is. If this passage challenges us to take our sin to God and repent it boldly, then, for heaven's sake, let's stop moaning about what he has or hasn't done and get on with it.

Have you been involved in an adulterous affair or are you on the verge of being unfaithful? Stand up straight or kneel right down and tell God that you have done wrong and you are sorry. Do it for him and for the wife or husband of your youth. Do it boldly.

Have you turned away from Jesus and allowed other things to become the gods in your life? Have you been unfaithful in that way? You will know if you have. Spit it out. You'll feel much better afterwards.

Reflection

Thinking about repentance is often much tougher than actually doing it. Won't it be good to feel clean again?

AP

MALACHI 2:17—3:3 (NIV)

Fire and soap

You have wearied the Lord with your words. 'How have we wearied him?' you ask. By saying, 'All who do evil are good in the eyes of the Lord, and he is pleased with them' or 'Where is the God of justice?' 'See, I will send my messenger, who will prepare the way before me. Then suddenly the Lord you are seeking will come to his temple; the messenger of the covenant, whom you desire, will come,' says the Lord Almighty. But who can endure the day of his coming? Who can stand when he appears? For he will be like a refiner's fire or a launderer's soap. He will sit as a refiner and purifier of silver; he will purify the Levites and refine them like gold and silver.

What an appalling notion it is that we might be wearying God with our words. Far worse than making him angry, don't you think? Just imagine it, God slumped on his heavenly throne, chin resting on one hand, bleary-eyed with the sheer tedium of listening to Adrian Plass moaning yet again about what's wrong with the world.

'It's not fair! All this following and trying to be good and pretending to like all the people at church and where does it get me? Can anyone tell me where it gets me? Don't bother. I'll tell you. Nowhere! That's where it gets me. In the meantime all the non-Christians get to lie in on Sunday morning while they plan their next batch of juicy weekend sins. I ask you—what is the point?'

I really don't want to weary God with my moaning, but I have to admit that I do descend into a sort of pit of miserable complaints from time to time. The threat of fire and soap is quite an effective one—imagine being scalded and scrubbed into the right frame of mind! The fact is, though, that I have become a son of God because of what Jesus did and, in my heart of hearts, his approval is what I really crave. Come on, my fellow moaners, let's allow that to be our motivation for coming to our senses. That should bring a smile to our Father's face.

Prayer

Father, forgive us for moaning. You have done so much for us and we are grateful.

AP

God's agenda

Then the Lord will have men who will bring offerings in righteousness, and the offerings of Judah and Jerusalem will be acceptable to the Lord, as in days gone by, as in former years. 'So I will come near to you for judgment. I will be quick to testify against sorcerers, adulterers and perjurers, against those who defraud labourers of their wages, who oppress the widows and the fatherless, and deprive aliens of justice, but do not fear me,' says the Lord Almighty. 'I the Lord do not change. So you, O descendants of Jacob, are not destroyed. Ever since the time of your forefathers you have turned away from my decrees and have not kept them. Return to me, and I will return to you,' says the Lord Almighty.

This list of sinful behaviour indicates the breadth and depth of God's social and spiritual agenda for the Church. It hasn't changed much. Concerns such as fair pay, proper treatment of foreigners and the oppression of vulnerable members of the community are as important to the heart of God today as they ever were, so they need to be just as important to us. In addition, within the Church itself, we urgently need to find the courage to weed out such issues as adultery and deliberate distortion of the truth so that we can turn to God with clean hearts and say, 'Here we are. We've returned. Please return to us.'

Don't misunderstand me. Not for one moment am I implying that there should be some sort of frenetic witch-hunt resulting in the detection and expulsion of wrong-doers. If all the sinners were to be removed from our church, for instance, Sunday mornings would be very quiet affairs. There would be no congregation and, let us be realistic, no vicar.

No, much more to the point is that we re-establish our corporate view of these matters and thus make it easier for all of us to see our behaviour in the context of responsible teaching and guidance. We don't want to lose our brothers and sisters—we want to keep them. Let the options be crystal clear and let us encourage each other to make the right choices. God will help us with that.

Prayer

Father, help us to teach your standards and measure ourselves honestly against them.

AP

Treasure from heaven

'But you ask, "How are we to return?" Will a man rob God? Yet you rob me. But you ask, "How do we rob you?" In tithes and offerings. You are under a curse—the whole nation of you—because you are robbing me. Bring the whole tithe into the storehouse, that there may be food in my house. Test me in this,' says the Lord Almighty, 'and see if I will not throw open the floodgates of heaven and pour out so much blessing that you will not have room enough for it. I will prevent pests from devouring your crops, and the vines in your fields will not cast their fruit,' says the Lord Almighty. 'Then all the nations will call you blessed, for yours will be a delightful land,' says the Lord Almighty.

Predictably, this is a favourite passage for those who teach that God showers material benefits on Christians who respond appropriately. At its worst, the 'appropriate response' involves parting with a far greater percentage of income than is actually sensible. A friend in Sweden got caught up in this nonsense. He was paying out such huge sums of money every month that his wife had trouble feeding the family with what remained. After three tortured years, the expected shower of benefits had failed to materialize and the marriage collapsed in a storm of bitter acrimony. An extreme example, but hardly an isolated one. The path of greed disguised as virtue is ominously broad. Most of us fail to give enough financially, but do you believe that God will provide a sort of lump sum benefit when we do increase the cash payments? Don't hold your breath.

No, let us give generously from what we have, but we know the wealth that Jesus promises is treasure in heaven, while the deposit, the shower of blessings that we receive in this life, is the peace of being in his will and pleasure. I tell myself that I would give anything for that, but the requirement is greater than mere money. God wants to sit on the throne of our hearts and have the very best of us available for him. Am I willing to pay that price? Hmmm…

Prayer

Open my heart, Lord.
Fill me with you.

AP

Conversation as prayer

'You have said harsh things against me,' says the Lord. 'Yet you ask, "What have we said against you?" You have said, "It is futile to serve God. What did we gain by carrying out his requirements and going about like mourners before the Lord Almighty? But now we call the arrogant blessed. Certainly the evildoers prosper, and even those who challenge God escape."' Then those who feared the Lord talked with each other, and the Lord listened and heard. A scroll of remembrance was written in his presence concerning those who feared the Lord and honoured his name. 'They will be mine,' says the Lord Almighty, 'in the day when I make up my treasured possession. I will spare them, just as in compassion a man spares his son who serves him. And you will again see the distinction between the righteous and the wicked, between those who serve God and those who do not.'

Theoretically, we improve as we get older. The theory holds good for me in certain areas. For instance, I have finally learned how to make the cardboard flap on top of a cereal packet fit into the little slot on the other side. I am proud of this.

In other areas I do not improve. I deteriorate. Take prayer. Private prayer is fine: I'm always nattering on to God. Nor do I mind formal, liturgical prayer: much of it is elegant and meaningful, and I love it. No, my problem is with extemporary prayer in small groups. Nowadays, my brain gets scrambled and my tongue ties itself in knots—it's horrible. Maybe after years spent consciously performing in these situations I doubt the integrity of my utterances. It's not

just that, though. There is also a growing awareness that prayer is, or can be, a much broader and richer experience than I had realized. As this passage suggests, conversation that is honestly and devoutly dedicated to God is heard by him as though it were prayer. These people feared the Lord and wanted to put things right. They talked together and God, having listened to what they said, got a secretarial angel to take down their names.

A thought

Obviously all kinds of prayer can be good and useful, but perhaps every word that we say should be an expression of ourselves to God.

AP

After the furnace

'Surely the day is coming; it will burn like a furnace. All the arrogant and every evildoer will be stubble, and that day that is coming will set them on fire,' says the Lord Almighty. 'Not a root or a branch will be left to them. But for you who revere my name, the sun of righteousness will rise with healing in its wings. And you will go out and leap like calves released from the stall. Then you will trample down the wicked; they will be ashes under the soles of your feet on the day when I do these things,' says the Lord Almighty.

I have no desire to trample on the wicked—well, not many of them—but if this means that one day we will trample on the negative things that make our lives imperfect, then I am all for it. Having said this, in my more pessimistic moods I wonder how much of me will be left after the furnace phase. I don't know about you, but nowadays my concerns are less about more obvious sins in my life than about the fact that I so often arrive at the end of the day with a feeling that mine has been a very thin performance.

Two things help to combat these gloomy moods. One is the constantly self-refreshing fact that Jesus is on my side and represents me to his Father with more passionate eloquence than I can ever command. Thank goodness for that. The other is that I am learning to place myself, by an effort of will, within God's view of the world through my eyes. Do these words mean anything? Well, they do, actually. Here's an example. Shopping needs doing. As I walk into the supermarket, I give the whole experience to God. Every tiny contact with any other person—in fact, every aspect of the time I spend there—will be put into his charge. Sounds silly? Maybe it is, but, on the occasions when I stir myself up to do it, there are interesting consequences.

In the end, it won't be about what we have done for God, but what he has managed to do through us. The furnace won't be able to touch that.

Prayer

Father, help us to concentrate on what you do instead of focusing on our own inadequacies.

AP

Healing in relationships

'Remember the law of my servant Moses, the decrees and laws I gave him at Horeb for all Israel. See, I will send you the prophet Elijah before that great and dreadful day of the Lord comes. He will turn the hearts of the fathers to their children, and the hearts of the children to their fathers; or else I will come and strike the land with a curse.'

Turn to chapter 11 of Matthew's Gospel and you will be able to hear Jesus explaining that this promise of a returning Elijah was eventually fulfilled in the ministry of John the Baptist. John was the cousin of Jesus, sent by God to prepare a way for the Messiah. He was a tough, straight-talking sort of guy who, if he had shared a bag of honey and locust-flavoured crisps in the corner of a pub with Malachi, would have discovered that the two of them had much in common as far as their message to Israel was concerned. They both called the people of God back into the place that was fundamentally right for them, a place where God's laws were observed and respected and the atmosphere around creator and creation could approximate to a paradise that was long lost.

Interesting, isn't it, to see that Malachi signs out on a note of healing in relationships. Parents to children, children to parents, generation to generation, God to man,

man to God. Both John and Malachi had a great deal to say about the specifics of conduct, but, for both of them, it was all a means to the same end—that end being the harmony of personalities relating to each other as they were supposed to from the beginning of time.

For many people, this is one of the most difficult things to understand about Christianity. Faith in Jesus is not about being seduced or drawn away to some ephemeral sphere that has no connection with what is real and central to human life. On the contrary, it is a means of returning to the granular, godly heart of existence. In other words—as Jesus himself explained so clearly—it is an invitation to come home.

Sunday prayer

Father, knowing you as we were meant to is a light in the far distance for most of us.
Lead us forward.

AP

The BRF
Magazine

Richard Fisher writes...

BRF has three core ministries—prayer and spirituality, discipleship and Bible reading—which together reflect our statement of purpose: 'resourcing your spiritual journey'. We've decided now to take each of our core ministries in turn as the theme for *The BRF Magazine*. So, in this issue we explore prayer and spirituality, in May we'll look at discipleship, and in September Bible reading. BRF is about so much more than just Bible reading notes!

Spirituality: the spiritual search; the search for meaning and fulfilment; the sense that 'there must be more to life than this...' All around us, both within the church and beyond, people are searching to make sense of their lives. Most people recognize that there is a spiritual dimension to our being. One of the fastest-growing sectors of secular bookshops is 'Mind, Body, Spirit' where you will find a plethora of books expounding and promoting a bewildering range of spiritualities, remedies and new age solutions to 'life, the universe, and everything'.

At BRF we're trying to help people who are searching for a deeper spirituality. We're concerned that those who are seeking should encounter Christian spirituality, rather than any of the weird and wonderful alternatives. We're concerned to help Christians who want to go further and deeper in their relationship with God. We're

concerned to 'minister to the ministers'—to support and resource church leaders and teachers for their own spirituality, when they are giving out so much of themselves in their ministry. 'Lord, teach us to pray,' said the disciples to Jesus. Another aspect of our ministry here at BRF is to provide resources to help people to explore different aspects of and approaches to prayer. After all, most of us need help with our prayer lives.

And so in the following pages we reflect something of BRF's core ministry of prayer and spirituality. We hope that you enjoy this new approach to *The BRF Magazine* and that you will find your own thinking and reflection stimulated and challenged.

Richard Fisher, Chief Executive

Quiet Spaces: exploring prayer and spirituality

In 2005 BRF launched a new spirituality journal, to be published in March, July and November each year. *Quiet Spaces*, with its 'dip-in' collection of articles, poems, meditations and prayers, offers access to a wealth of material from a range of Christian traditions, to enrich your walk with God and help you live out your faith in everyday life. Each issue focuses on a single theme, the first three volumes covering 'Creation and creativity', 'The journey' and 'The feast'. The next issue, available from March 2006, will be devoted to 'The garden'. The extract below is taken from *Quiet Spaces: The Journey* and is written by Julie Watson, who, in March 2004, joined a trek through the Sinai desert.

The desert speaks

Welcome, travellers, welcome. Welcome to my world, for I am the desert in which you walk, following in the footsteps of thousands —seekers, pilgrims, runaways. However you arrived here, welcome.

I am old and shaped by wind and water, silent, empty and barren. I am the place that few seek, yet many find; for those who are driven to journey here are unaware that in the silence their own souls will shout more loudly. I have watched many journey across rock and sand, and seen their joy and tears. None can be unaffected by their time here, whether alone or with friends; each is silenced by the awesome power of the empti-ness or perhaps simply by the absence of their usual busy world.

Let me share with you some of my memories as I have watched the passing of time.

Long, long ago, a whole people passed through this desert—the children of Israel, a whole mass of humanity wandering after their God. Eventually they left the desert and entered their own land. Many years later I overheard another group: travelling from the east, they watched the night skies, seeking a special star that signified the birth of a great king. Soon after these magi, a young couple and their tiny baby passed through to hide in Egypt for a time, escaping a massacre, and when it was safe they returned home. Many have come over the years by choice or compulsion, journeying for a few days or weeks, months or even years, learning the wisdom of the desert.

Today another group has entered the land. They are eager and keen to explore, but how will they manage as the desert begins to explore each one of them? They begin at speed but soon slow down as solid rock turns to soft, flowing sand—two steps forward and one slide back. Faced by a huge sand dune, some are overwhelmed. Tantrum Hill, it has been named by those who wrestled with themselves to complete the challenge, for there is no way forward except to climb the dune; and even in a group, each person faces it alone. Some approach with quiet determination, others with tears and tantrums. They climb, finding that when they reach what appeared to be the top, another dune awaits. Time slows as they crawl ahead, then stand speechless at the top, for it is only there that the beauty of my presence is revealed and they clearly see the brown barren ground and the bright blue of the sky. For here there is no vegetation to mask the underlying rock and so the desert brings each one to face themselves and who they really are. Only now can they begin to understand the struggle and purpose of this journey.

Watching them descend slowly once again from the high peaks to the dry valleys, I wonder whether they will settle tonight. The thoughts that they have had will roll around in their minds, and sleep will be hard to find. The ground is hard too: lumps of granite protrude through the thin mattresses that they are trying to sleep on. In their sleeplessness, perhaps they will look up to the heavens around them and see the wonders encapsulated in the desert skies. For in the deep darkness stars have appeared, as if a child has sprinkled silver glitter over a huge expanse of thick black velvet. So many can be seen tonight that they are amazed, yet those stars have been above them every night of their lives. Before, they were in places filled with light, with comfortable beds and pleasant dreams; but now, in the deepest desert, the night reveals the beauty of the starlit darkness. They will remember this night, and that hidden things are as real as those that can be seen and known.

Weary, they wake, wondering

Many pass through the desert without leaving footprints, for their journey is deep within themselves

who chose for them to come this way, facing another day of walking —today down a wadi, a dry riverbed. After a time they will think that they have seen enough of sand and rock and that the desert is truly barren; then they will be surprised by flowers blossoming where they are least expected. Even in the deepest desert there is life, not as obvious as in their other world, for here water is scarce and hidden underground, a treasure of more value than gold. Plants and trees grow, their roots seeking a suggestion of water, growing towards the place that will give them life, deeper and deeper, building strong foundations for growth, reaching up to the sunshine and the highest heavens. Here the trees provide rest for weary travellers, a small pool of shade from the burning sun, an oasis of peace in the challenge of the journey.

Soon they will enter my gallery —sculptures made from sandstone, eroded by wind and water day by day cutting through sand that became stone, to return it to sand again and so complete the cycle. They have walked through the desert being surprised by awesome views, becoming aware of their weaknesses and the strength of their endurance; they have huddled into corners and tried to hide behind rocks; they have stood on the highest peaks and rejoiced in their own being. Soon they will leave the desert and be confronted once again by colour and noise and the busyness of the life they left behind, but they will never be the same again, for they have passed through the furnace of the desert and have been changed for ever.

Many pass through the desert without leaving footprints, for their journey is deep within themselves. Many fear finding the darkest night of the desert. But do not be afraid, my travellers, for I welcome you; and if you dare to embrace the desert, you will find riches beyond your wildest dreams.

Julie Watson is a minister in secular employment, working full-time as a Principal Lecturer at the University of Teesside and serving as Assistant Curate in Redcar.

Commendation for *Quiet Spaces* from The Revd Canon David Adam:

What a joy to have Quiet Spaces *and its offer of ways of journeying into the awareness of the Power, Peace and Presence of God... Let those who risk taking 'time out' to read* Quiet Spaces *be filled with the wonder, awe and beauty of what God presents to them each day.*

To order any of the Quiet Spaces *volumes or to subscribe regularly, please turn to the order forms on pages 158 and 159. You can also visit the website: www.quietspaces.org.uk.*

Michael Mitton

FOREWORD BY DAVID PYTCHES

the
Rainbow
of renewal

Daily Bible reflections for Lent and Easter

An extract from
The Rainbow of Renewal

This book of daily readings for Lent and Easter explores how the transforming power of God, through the work of the Holy Spirit, can bring renewal to each one of us. Different aspects of renewal are linked to colours of the rainbow, because rainbows are the essence of light. When the white light of God is projected through the prism of our lives, all the colours of renewal are revealed. The author is the Revd Michael Mitton, Project Officer for Renewing Ministry in the Derby Diocese. He has also written *A Heart to Listen* for BRF. The following extract is the reading for Ash Wednesday.

Exiles in Babylon

By the rivers of Babylon—there we sat down and there we wept when we remembered Zion. On the willows there we hung up our harps. For there our captors asked us for songs, and our tormentors asked for mirth, saying, 'Sing us one of the songs of Zion!' How could we sing the Lord's song in a foreign land? If I forget you, O Jerusalem, let my right hand wither! Let my tongue cling to the roof of my mouth, if I do not remember you, if I do not set Jerusalem above my highest joy. Remember, O Lord, against the Edomites the day of Jerusalem's fall, how they said, 'Tear it down! Tear it down! Down to its foundations!' O daughter Babylon, you devastator! Happy shall they be who pay you back what you have done to us! Happy shall they be who take your little ones and dash them against the rock! (Psalm 137)

This psalm gives us an insight into a most devastating experience of corporate grief. When Joshua triumphantly marched the faithful people of God into the Promised Land, the future looked wonderful. God had rescued his people from Egypt; he had led them through the wilderness, and they then enjoyed an era of occupying the land that had been promised to them right at the beginning of their story of faith (Genesis 12:7). In time, God granted them their wish of having a king, and David was the one chosen for the task.

However, it was not long before David's descendants erred and strayed into just about every type of offence imaginable, and the kingdom became increasingly vulnerable to foreign invaders, as God withdrew his protection from the rebellious people. Eventually the unthinkable happened: a foreign people invaded Jerusalem; the mighty temple, which looked so indestructible, was pulled down; the king was blinded and led pathetically to imprisonment, and much of the population was marched ignominiously out of the city on another desert walk, this time not to the Holy Land, but away from it to Babylon.

So it was that they found themselves as refugees in a foreign land, where nothing was familiar, their faith was disregarded, and they were treated like slaves. Worst of all, God seemed to have abandoned them. They had believed he would preserve Jerusalem no matter what, and yet when it came to the crunch, he was apparently nowhere to be seen.

Thus, a group of them find themselves slumped down by the waters of Babylon, and all they can do is to think back to the good old days of Zion. Babylon was very different to Judea: it had an intricate system of canals, running across a huge, flat plain, which would have felt so different to the hills and valleys of Judea. They sit down by one of these canals and chat together, and one of them might say, 'Do you remember how at this time of year, we would go up to the temple to make our offering, go through that mighty gate and hear the sound of the busy market, and listen to the prayers of the priest...' Others may join in, until it becomes too painful to continue. Each time they remember, they weep. It is what grieving people do. Those who have lost people they love want to recall many memories. We say, 'Do you remember how he used to...', 'Do you remember she loved to...', and it is a sort of bittersweet experience. We feel comforted by the remembrance, and yet it often brings tears, as we are aware of the extent of our loss.

They found themselves refugees in a foreign land

The people of God in Babylon are no longer able to sing, and so they hang up their lyres. How painful it must have been when the captors taunted them, saying, 'Go on, sing us one of those odd songs you used to sing back in Jerusalem.' These were songs full of meaning and emotion for the Judeans, but for the Babylonians they were a source of mockery.

But the psalm tells us that these people of God, though deeply grieving, had an impressive stubbornness. Their inability to sing in a strange land does not mean they will forget Jerusalem—far from it. They may not understand, but they will hang on to hope. They'd sooner lose their hands and their tongues than forget Jerusalem. The psalm ends with terrible words that we find almost impossible to read—the vengeful killing of innocent children makes us think of callous terrorist blasts that are all too familiar in our day. There is deep hatred of the perpetrators of exile here, and the mourners give themselves strength in the only way they know how, which is to spit out venomous threats at their captors.

I have no idea what it must be like to be led away from a home and people I love and be taken to a land where all the customs and cultures are quite alien to me, where I cannot communicate because I don't know the language, and the people amongst whom I live view me with suspicion and distaste. I am all too aware that in this often sad and violent world that experience is far too common, and the issue of asylum seekers in 21st-century Britain is alerting us to the problems and pains of refugees. But for most of us this kind of exile is not something we are likely to experience personally. Nonetheless, it is quite possible to know a very deep sense of corporate loss at a way of life that once we took for granted, but now seems a million miles away.

The film adaptation of the first book of *The Lord of the Rings* begins with a mysterious voice narrating the words: 'The world has changed. I feel it in the water; I feel it in the earth; I smell it in the air. Much that once was is lost, for none now live who remember it.' The rest of the dramatic story builds upon the fact that things have taken place that have deeply disturbed the world, and no one really understands or remembers how it was, or how we got to this point. There are many in our churches who may feel this way: 'The church has changed… much that once was is lost.' There are people in the church where I serve who have been part of the congregation all their lives. They are in their 70s and 80s, and they have seen many different phases in the life of the church. They readily look back at the days when the building was full, the choir-stalls full of enthusiastic choristers of all ages, the Sunday School thriving, and the takings at the parish bazaar enough to cover the church costs. Now they look round at a society that has all but turned its back on God; they see that few churches have their own clergy, but have to share them with other churches; they witness clergy ignoring so many of the traditions that were once hallowed. Much that once was is lost. By the waters of the 21st-century post-modern, texting, Big-Brother-watching, eBay-shopping world, they sit down and weep.

Of course, it is not just the elderly who have this experience. Any of us can drive around this land and see once large churches in urban and rural situations now struggling with dwindling congregations, battling with the ever-increasing financial burdens of leaking roofs and crumbling walls, and we too can find ourselves thinking back to the good old days when churches looked very successful. We too can feel the dull ache of despair afflicting our souls.

And yet, paradoxically, this experience can be the beginning of renewal. For the people described in the psalm, their response was anger against the perpetrators of the humiliation and destruction that they had suffered. Today, in our longing for renewal, we can also easily end up with a 'blame' mentality, so that we look for those whom we can hold responsible for getting us into this situation. Others during that time of exile would have just shrugged their shoulders and said in effect, 'Oh well, this is now how it is. Let's settle down here in Babylon.' But thankfully there were prophets around who gave an inspiring lead to help people move from despair to hope and, in time, to make a journey of renewal to build a new Jerusalem. We shall look at this a bit more tomorrow, but today's task is to acknowledge how we feel about the losses that we have experienced individually and corporately in connection with the life of the church. You may be part of a church that once was alive in many ways, but now things have gone quiet and dry; you may once have belonged to a church that seemed so alive, but where you are now feels as if it lacks life by comparison; you may have left your church because you were disappointed with it, and now you live your Christian life more or less alone. Or maybe it is not your personal experience that bothers you, but you have a sense of connection with the wider community of the Church, and you grieve because in some areas of its life it has experienced many losses. If, on the other hand, you are in a church that is ablaze with renewal, then give thanks to God (and say a prayer for those who envy what you have).

Reflection

Think about your church situation—is it one of renewal at the moment? If it is, where do you see the renewal expressing itself? If not, what are your feelings about its situation? What is in your heart as you reflect on this? Grief? Blaming? Reluctant acceptance? Longing for the old days? Hope? You might like to try writing a psalm to express your feelings, making it your prayer to God.

Prayer

Lord, today is the beginning of Lent, and I choose to journey with you in these coming days. Only you know where you will lead me. Give me all that I need to let go of all that would weigh me down, and to be open to the new things you want to show me. Lead me by the waters of renewal.

To order a copy of this book, please turn to the order form on page 159.

Holy Travelling

Deborah and David Douglas

When people went on pilgrimage in the Middle Ages, it was usually a matter of penance and indulgences: journeys to distant shrines might procure a saint's favour or subtract years from Purgatory. The renewed interest in pilgrimage among Christians of all denominations, however, has more to do with deepening a sense of the real presence of God in our lives. Contemporary pilgrimage, as the Anglican writer Evelyn Underhill once noted of spiritual retreat, 'puts in the foreground and keeps in the foreground that which is, after all, the first interest of religion: the soul's relation to God'.

Pilgrims, unlike tourists, tend to travel light. They have sloughed off daily distractions in exchange for prayerful attentiveness. Jesus promised his disciples that 'the Holy Spirit will bring to your remembrance all that I have said to you', and holy travelling often provides the ground for holy recollection.

On the map of Christianity, some places seem to draw visitors more powerfully than others. Scotland's Isle of Iona, for George MacLeod and others, has proved a 'thin place—only a tissue paper separating earth from heaven'. Such 'thin places', by means of their landscape, architecture, history and even weather, can evoke in travellers a sense of expectancy and clarity, and help to mediate the presence and grace of God. Just as there have been particularly credi-

ble evangelists down the centuries, it's not surprising that there exist particularly credible witnesses of place.

But, at the same time, contemporary pilgrims keep in mind Evelyn Underhill's observation that 'from our human point of view some places are a great deal thinner than others: but to the eyes of worship the whole of the visible world, even its most unlikely patches, is rather "thin"'. Indeed, as Elizabeth Barrett Browning noted, 'Earth's crammed with heaven / And every common bush afire with God'.

Moreover, what draws pilgrims closer to God is not only the physical destination, but the people associated with it. In our own travels across Britain, as we researched and wrote our book, *Pilgrims in the Kingdom*, we discovered that what began with places led inexorably to the brave, visionary, joyful people who lived there—some in hermit caves and windswept islands, others in medieval monasteries or Victorian towns. We found that one of the great and unexpected gifts of pilgrimage was this expanded sense of the communion of saints.

Britain is uniquely rich in places to meet these heroes of the Christian faith. Both across time—from fourth-century mission centres to Coventry Cathedral's 21st-century ministry of reconciliation—and across Celtic, Catholic, Anglican and Protestant traditions, there are few better lands in the world, these two grateful Americans believe, to experience the wealth of Christendom's people and places.

Our years of exploration allowed us to sojourn in the landscape of Saint Ninian at Whithorn, and Saints Aidan and Cuthbert at Lindisfarne, and to glimpse the martyrdom sites of Thomas Becket in Canterbury and Margaret Clitherow in York. We understood more clearly the acts of faith carried out with humility and courage by Queen Margaret of Scotland, Lady Julian of Norwich and Nicholas Ferrar of Little Gidding.

We included in our book not only renowned pilgrimage destinations, but less traditional sites—such as John Wesley's Aldersgate Street (where he had 'felt his heart strangely warmed'), George Fox's Pendle Hill, and Evelyn Underhill's retreat house at Pleshey, where men and women had directly experienced God's love and conveyed that possibility to others. We were immeasurably enriched as a result of travelling in the footsteps of such writers of faith as George Herbert in Bemerton, John Newton in Olney, Gerard Manley Hopkins at St Bueno's, and C.S. Lewis in Oxford.

T.S. Eliot honoured the chapel at Little Gidding as a place 'where prayer has been valid'. As we knelt there and in similar settings, we discovered that these journeys had led less to a gathering of historical information or a satisfaction of curiosity than to a strengthening of our lives in God.

For us, learning to pay attention in these places helped us to pay attention everywhere, to put ourselves daily in landscapes where we remain oriented towards God. We have found ourselves, in significant times of decision, thinking of these fellow pilgrims, remembering their faith and hope, and being fortified by their witness.

We can, by grace, return from pilgrimage sites with a heart open to the people who prayed there and to the God to whom they prayed—a possibility of transformation so profound as to be sacramental. When one has knelt where prayer has been valid, one rarely rises again quite the same.

Pilgrims in the Kingdom *was published by BRF in 2004. To order a copy, please turn to the order form on page 159.*

BRF's Prayer and Spirituality Range

Naomi Starkey

As part of BRF's aim of resourcing people on their spiritual journey, no matter what stage they may be at, we publish a range of books that take as their focus different aspects of prayer and spirituality. These books complement our Bible reading notes and *Quiet Spaces* journal, by taking a more in-depth and systematic look at a whole range of themes to do with our relationship with God.

Interest in the general area of 'spirituality' has grown enormously over recent years, with many people aware of the importance of refreshing the soul as well as exercising the body. They are often equally aware of how hard it can be to do either, in the busyness of modern life. In building our Prayer and Spirituality range, we want to help people develop a Christian spirituality that is rooted in the Bible, watered by the Holy Spirit and nourished by fellowship with other believers.

Our books are divided into three main categories, to make it easier to identify which title would be most helpful for a particular need or situation. The categories are teaching about prayer; ways of praying; spiritual reading.

In our 'teaching about prayer' category, we include books that give helpful advice, often drawn from the author's own experience, about how to pray, even if you have never tried it before. *Long Wandering Prayer* by David Hansen is just such a book. It shows how prayer can take place just as easily on a long walk (and sometimes more so) as kneeling or sitting behind a closed door or even in a church. The author encourages us to let go of the drive to control our thoughts and offers advice on how to practise simply *being* in the presence of the living God.

In this same category, *Seeking God's Face* by Beryl Adamsbaum is a short and accessible little book that considers in straightforward terms why prayer is important, how to pray and stay grounded in scripture, how to grow in confidence as we approach and communicate with God, and what to do when God seems silent. A new study guide to accompany this book can be found on the BRF website.

Our 'ways of praying' category provides helpful material that can provide a way of getting started (or going deeper) in prayer. John Henstridge's *Transforming the Ordinary* offers a series of prayer meditations based around Bible passages that can transform the routines of daily life into moments to tune into God's presence. The meditations can be used by individuals and also in a group setting, and the book's introduction suggests ways of doing this.

A World of Prayer takes a different approach, presenting a globe-spanning collection of material that can be used for prayer and praise. It is compiled from the liturgies specially written for the annual services of Women's World Day of Prayer. Representing ten countries from Guatemala to Indonesia, the book includes worship material on a range of themes, such as caring for our world, healing and wholeness, and responding to God's call.

In our 'spiritual reading' category, we branch out from the act of praying itself, to considering how we relate to God both as individuals and as church communities, including how we can draw encouragement from less familiar parts of the Church as well as inspiring figures from Christian history. These are books designed to help people grow in faith through various life experiences, which celebrate the life and worship of the Church, and which offer essential fuel for the journey of discipleship.

The Flame of Sacred Love has been a popular title in this category for a number of years, selling nearly 6,000 copies to date. Written by the late Brother Ramon, a Franciscan hermit, it is an ideal introduction to the practice of contemplative prayer. Based around themes from the popular Charles Wesley hymn 'O thou who camest from above', it explores spiritual riches from across the Christian spiritual traditions—Orthodox, Catholic and Anglican. As well as teaching about spirituality, it also includes helpful prayer exercises that will provoke thought and stimulate the mind and heart to growth.

Taking the 'life experiences' theme, Wendy Bray's *In the Palm of God's Hand* is based on her personal prayer diary, written as she struggled with severe, long-term illness. Winner of the 2002 Biography of the Year at the Christian Book Awards, Wendy Bray's honest, moving and, incredibly, often funny account shows how personal faith can transform even the hardest of times and that God's love and mercy can still break through, no matter how tough the situation.

These are, of course, just a selection from the full Prayer and Spirituality range. To find out more about these books, and about the others we publish in this area, do visit our website: www.brf.org.uk.

Sounding the Retreat

Martyn Payne

So, you're from *Barnabas* too. You know, Lucy was *so* good last year!' This is not the first time I have been greeted with words like these on my travels. I just have to hope I can somehow follow in my colleague's glorious footsteps.

The occasion was the Chichester Diocesan Children's Leaders' annual retreat, deep in the Sussex countryside near Lewes. A number of the leaders were regular attendees, who really look forward to this break from routine, which includes some beautiful countryside walks, plenty of time to relax and chat, sessions exploring God's word together and worship.

Our Friday evening to Sunday afternoon experience fell within the ten days between Ascension and Pentecost. For the followers of Jesus in that upper room, this was a time of waiting, praying and getting ready for the next stage of their work. It was easy, therefore, for us to be there in our imaginations and join the 120 that gathered at different times and who must have shared their stories and experiences of Jesus' ministry with each other.

We stepped in among those storytellers in Jerusalem and looked again at some of the incidents in John's Gospel in particular. We followed the beloved disciple's own prologue by trying to make sure that the 'Word became flesh' for us, so that we could fall in love with the story afresh. How else will we be able to share and be good news to the children we work with?

The tone of the sessions was conversational and reflective, using symbols and some *Godly Play* style presentations. All this, along with the powerful worship, splendid meals, fun and games, walks and plenty of laughter, played a vital part in restoring our souls.

This ministry really is an important but often neglected piece of the spiritual diet for those who work week-by-week faithfully and creatively with children. I would strongly recommend that churches consider Quiet Days or retreats as a way of resourcing their children's leaders. If you are interested in organizing one with *Barnabas*, then please be in touch. Sounding the retreat is certainly the way forward!

To support BRF's ministry with children, please see the form on page 156.

Children's spirituality

Kathryn Copsey

One of my most memorable encounters with children took place one Sunday afternoon in a church on an outer urban estate. A small group of about 30 of us were meeting for a regular Sunday afternoon service. The theme for the Sunday was Jesus' attitude to children: 'Unless you change and become like children you will never enter the kingdom of heaven.' Suddenly there was a scraping and scrabbling at the back of the church. The door flew open and the peace of the service was shattered by two boys of about nine or ten skimming up the side aisle of the church on rollerblades!

'Hello,' said the minister. 'Here, have a seat. You're just in time to help me with my talk.' He drew the giggling, half-embarrassed boys into the welcoming arms of the circle of people, and carried on. Then it was time for the prayers. Who said it was best to pray with your eyes shut? 'Psst,' said my neighbour. 'Better get those boys to empty their pockets.' While we'd been praying, they had helped themselves to the votive candle money sitting temptingly near. You had to admire their timing!

I must be honest: there was a sinking feeling in the pit of my stomach. We were a fragile group of people, some with mental health needs, others with learning disabilities. The last thing we needed were two lively boys making mischief. But the welcome and understanding offered by the others in the group (people who had no agenda about power and being 'adult', but identified with the marginal status of the children) made me realize yet again how we need constantly to allow Jesus' attitude to children to touch us and his words to transform us.

We need constantly to allow Jesus' attitude to children to touch us

I wrote *From the Ground Up* (BRF, 2005) to share a little of my journey alongside children, to invite others to catch a glimpse of their rich spiritual world, and to share the thinking underlying CURBS (Children in URBan Situations), the charity that I have the privilege of leading. It is written against the background of a society that, with the intention of raising levels of 'success', is squeezing space for reflection, for nurturing a sense of awe and wonder, for music and art, for simple 'time to be', out of the curriculum. It is written at a time when 'yobs' are demonized, curfews are imposed, ASBOs are served on ever younger children, and the rise in under-16 pregnancies is a cause for concern. It is written when 'spirituality' is a buzz word featuring in the National Curriculum, yet in practice seems to be little understood. These are the experiences of many of the children we touch through CURBS.

The challenge for me is twofold:

- What new perspectives on the child do I glean from the Bible?
- What new truths about myself, about the child and about society can I learn from the child?

I am totally convinced that if we take this challenge seriously, recognizing the key importance of the child's early years, we will learn how to restore children's damaged spirituality. In doing this we will offer them a pattern for life that will run counter to the image society has accorded them—which some of them have earned!

I have worked with children who have no sense of their own self-worth, attach no value to their thoughts and ideas, do not trust their feelings, have no opportunity to learn to make good choices, experience no trustworthiness or consistency from the adults in their lives, and have never learned to handle anger or hatred constructively. Yet Genesis 1:26 tells us that every single child we meet is made in God's image. Every single child has a spiritual dimension, a spirituality. God is present in *every* child we meet— even the most damaged. Do we listen to the news about the yobs and think, 'God himself is there within that young person'?

In the chapters leading up to Matthew 18, the disciples were taken up with 'adult' issues to do with comfort, security, certainty, competitiveness and status. Jesus had obviously got his priorities wrong: he was teaching that he was on his way to die in Jerusalem. Into the middle of the disciples' arguments, Jesus places a child— probably just an ordinary child who would have been hovering

God is present in every child we meet— even the most damaged

around. Children I work with hover around: difficult kids, damaged kids, lonely kids, kids at a loose end. No doubt kids hovered around Jesus: children know when a grown-up has a child-friendly heart. They hovered around enjoying Jesus' company; they waited in anticipation to hear him speak or see what he would do; they were ready to run an errand; they were confident that Jesus would have time for them; unlike the disciples, they had no thought of being 'great', they simply lived in the moment.

If we take Genesis and Matthew seriously, our attitude to children must completely change. We will take it seriously that each child has an inborn spirituality and that, in welcoming the child, we welcome Christ. We will take it seriously that unless we change and become like children we will *not enter* the kingdom of heaven.

Within CURBS, we act on our conviction that each child is created in God's image, recognizing, however, that this image is damaged by the world in which we live—damaged both unintentionally and intentionally. We believe that we need to repair this damaged spirituality in order for it to become a springboard for faith. We repair spirituality by the attitudes we model as adults, by the nurturing environments we offer a child, by the activities we engage in with the child that allow for the exploration of choices, feelings, wonder,

emotions, trust and communication. Above all, we offer ourselves to the children through forming quality relationships with them, believing that God created us to be in relationship with others and with himself.

From the Ground Up invites us to walk through our world led by a child, and it challenges us to be transformed by the lessons learned on this walk.

For more information about CURBS, visit www.curbsproject.org.uk or email info@curbsproject.org.uk.

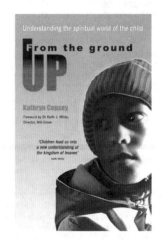

Kathryn Copsey is a trained community worker, and has worked with children for the past 30 years, mostly in urban situations such as East London. To order a copy of her book, From the Ground Up, *please turn to the order form on page 159.*

New Daylight © BRF 2006

The Bible Reading Fellowship
First Floor, Elsfield Hall, 15–17 Elsfield Way, Oxford OX2 8FG
Tel: 01865 319700; Fax: 01865 319701
E-mail: enquiries@brf.org.uk
Website: www.brf.org.uk

ISBN 1 84101 274 2

Distributed in Australia by:
Willow Connection, PO Box 288, Brookvale, NSW 2100.
Tel: 02 9948 3957; Fax: 02 9948 8153;
E-mail: info@willowconnection.com.au
Available also from all good Christian bookshops in Australia.
For individual and group subscriptions in Australia:
Mrs Rosemary Morrall, PO Box W35, Wanniassa, ACT 2903.

Distributed in New Zealand by:
Scripture Union Wholesale, PO Box 760, Wellington
Tel: 04 385 0421; Fax: 04 384 3990; E-mail: suwholesale@clear.net.nz

Distributed in the USA by:
The Bible Reading Fellowship, PO Box 380, Winter Park,
Florida 32790-0380
Tel: 407 628 4330 or 800 749 4331; Fax: 407 647 2406;
E-mail: brf@biblereading.org; Website: www.biblereading.org

Publications distributed to more than 60 countries

Acknowledgments

Printed in Singapore by Craft Print International Ltd

BRF is a Christian charity committed to resourcing the spiritual journey of adults and children alike. For adults, BRF publishes Bible reading notes and books and offers an annual programme of quiet days and retreats. Under its children's imprint *Barnabas*, BRF publishes a wide range of books for those working with children under 11 in school, church and home. BRF's *Barnabas Ministry* team offers INSET sessions for primary teachers, training for children's leaders in church, quiet days, and a range of events to enable children themselves to engage with the Bible and its message.

We need your help if we are to make a real impact on the local church and community. In an increasingly secular world people need even more help with their Bible reading, their prayer and their discipleship. We can do something about this, but our resources are limited. With your help, if we all do a little, together we can make a huge difference.

How can you help?

- You could support BRF's ministry with a donation or standing order (using the response form overleaf).

- You could consider making a bequest to BRF in your will, and so give lasting support to our work. (We have a leaflet available with more information about this, which can be requested using the form overleaf.)

- And, most important of all, you could support BRF with your prayers.

Whatever you can do or give, we thank you for your support.

BRF – resourcing your spiritual journey

BRF MINISTRY APPEAL RESPONSE FORM

Name _____

Address _____

_____ Postcode _____

Telephone _____ Email _____

(Please tick boxes as appropriate. Delete as applicable where marked *)

Gift Aid Declaration

❏ I am a UK taxpayer. I want BRF to treat as Gift Aid Donations all donations I make from 6 April 2000 until I notify you otherwise.

Signature _____ Date _____

❏ I would like to support BRF's adult/children's* ministry with a regular donation by standing order (please complete the Banker's Order below).

Standing Order – Banker's Order

To the Manager, Name of Bank/Building Society _____

Address _____

_____ Postcode _____

Sort Code _____ Account Name _____

Account No _____

Please pay Royal Bank of Scotland plc, London Drummonds Branch, 49 Charing Cross, London SW1A 2DX (Sort Code 16-00-38), for the account of BRF A/C No. 00774151

The sum of _____ pounds on ___ /___ /___ (insert date your standing order starts) and thereafter the same amount on the same day of each month until further notice.

Signature _____ Date _____

Single donation

❏ I enclose my cheque/credit card/Switch card details for a donation of
£5 £10 £25 £50 £100 (other) £_____ to support BRF's adult/children's* ministry)

Credit/ Switch card no. ☐☐☐☐☐☐☐☐☐☐☐☐☐☐☐☐☐☐☐☐

Expires ☐☐ ☐☐ ☐☐   Issue no. of Switch card ☐☐☐

Signature _____ Date _____

(Where appropriate, on receipt of your donation, we will send you a Gift Aid form)

❏ Please send me information about making a bequest to BRF in my will.

Please detach and send this completed form to: Richard Fisher, BRF, First Floor, Elsfield Hall, 15–17 Elsfield Way, Oxford OX2 8FG. BRF is a Registered Charity (No.233280)

ND0106

NEW DAYLIGHT SUBSCRIPTIONS

Please note our subscription rates 2006–2007. From the May 2006 issue, the new subscription rates will be:

Individual subscriptions covering 3 issues for under 5 copies, payable in advance (including postage and packing):

	UK	SURFACE	AIRMAIL
NEW DAYLIGHT each set of 3 p.a.	£12.00	£13.35	£15.60
NEW DAYLIGHT 3-year sub i.e. 9 issues	£29.55	N/A	N/A
(Not available for Large Print)			
NEW DAYLIGHT LGE PRINT each set of 3 p.a.	£16.80	£20.40	£24.90

Group subscriptions covering 3 issues for 5 copies or more, sent to ONE address (post free):

NEW DAYLIGHT	£10.05	each set of 3 p.a.
NEW DAYLIGHT LGE PRINT	£14.97	each set of 3 p.a.

Please note that the annual billing period for Group Subscriptions runs from 1 May to 30 April.

Copies of the notes may also be obtained from Christian bookshops:

NEW DAYLIGHT	£3.35 each copy
NEW DAYLIGHT LGE PRINT	£4.99 each copy

SUBSCRIPTIONS

❑ I would like to take out a subscription myself (complete your name and
address details only once)

❑ I would like to give a gift subscription (please complete both name and
address sections below)

Your name _____

Your address _____

_____ Postcode _____

Gift subscription name _____

Gift subscription address _____

_____ Postcode _____

Please send *New Daylight* beginning with the May / September 2006 /
January 07 issue: (delete as applicable)

(please tick box)	UK	SURFACE	AIR MAIL
NEW DAYLIGHT	❑ £12.00	❑ £13.35	❑ £15.60
NEW DAYLIGHT 3-year sub	❑ £29.55		
NEW DAYLIGHT LARGE PRINT	❑ £16.80	❑ £20.40	❑ £24.90

I would like to take out an annual subscription to *Quiet Spaces* beginning
with the next available issue:

(please tick box)	UK	SURFACE	AIR MAIL
QUIET SPACES	❑ £16.95	❑ £18.45	❑ £20.85

Please complete the payment details below and send your coupon, with
appropriate payment, to: **BRF, First Floor, Elsfield Hall, 15–17 Elsfield Way,
Oxford OX2 8FG.**

Total enclosed £ _____ (cheques should be made payable to 'BRF')

Payment by cheque ❑ postal order ❑ Visa ❑ Mastercard ❑ Switch ❑

Card number: ⬜⬜⬜⬜ ⬜⬜⬜⬜ ⬜⬜⬜⬜ ⬜⬜⬜⬜

Expiry date of card: ⬜⬜⬜⬜   Issue number (Switch): ⬜⬜⬜⬜

Signature (essential if paying by credit/Switch card) _____

❑ Please do not send me further information about BRF publications.

BRF resources are available from your local Christian bookshop. BRF is a Registered Charity

BRF PUBLICATIONS ORDER FORM

Please ensure that you complete and send off both sides of this order form.

Please send me the following book(s):

		Quantity	Price	Total
436 2	The Rainbow of Renewal (M. Mitton)	_____	£7.99	_____
269 6	A Heart to Listen (M. Mitton)	_____	£7.99	_____
265 3	Pilgrims in the Kingdom (D. & D. Douglas)	_____	£12.99	_____
386 2	From the Ground Up (K. Copsey)	_____	£6.99	_____
455 9	The Story of Easter (C. Doyle)	_____	£6.99	_____
456 7	Open the Door (V. Howie)	_____	£6.99	_____
026 X	Long Wandering Prayer (D. Hansen)	_____	£6.99	_____
370 6	Seeking God's Face (B. Adamsbaum)	_____	£4.99	_____
316 1	Transforming the Ordinary (J. Henstridge)	_____	£6.99	_____
369 2	A World of Prayer (ed. N. Starkey)	_____	£6.99	_____
037 5	The Flame of Sacred Love (Brother Ramon)	_____	£7.99	_____
336 6	In the Palm of God's Hand (W. Bray)	_____	£6.99	_____
237 8	The Music of Praise (G. Giles)	_____	£12.99	_____
334 X	The Harmony of Heaven (G. Giles)	_____	£7.99	_____
125 8	Strength of the Hills (J. Robertson)	_____	£5.99	_____
391 9	Old Words, New Life (D. Winter)	_____	£6.99	_____
291 2	Song of the Shepherd (T. Horsfall)	_____	£6.99	_____
126 6	Living the Gospel (Helen Julian CSF)	_____	£5.99	_____
322 6	The Lindisfarne Icon (Helen Julian CSF)	_____	£6.99	_____
3552 4	When You Walk (A. Plass)	_____	£8.99	_____

Total cost of books £ _____

Postage and packing (see over) £ _____

TOTAL £ _____

See over for payment details. All prices are correct at time of going to press, are subject to the prevailing rate of VAT and may be subject to change without prior warning.

BRF resources are available from your local Christian bookshop. BRF is a Registered Charity

PAYMENT DETAILS

Please complete the payment details below and send with appropriate payment and completed order form to:

**BRF, First Floor, Elsfield Hall,
15–17 Elsfield Way, Oxford OX2 8FG**

Name _____

Address _____

_____

_____ Postcode _____

Telephone _____

Email _____

Total enclosed £ _____(cheques should be made payable to 'BRF')

Payment by cheque ❑ postal order ❑ Visa ❑ Mastercard ❑ Switch ❑

Card number: ❑❑❑❑❑❑❑❑❑❑❑❑❑❑❑❑❑❑❑

Expiry date of card: ❑❑❑❑   Issue number (Switch): ❑❑❑❑

Signature (essential if paying by credit/Switch card) _____

ALTERNATIVE WAYS TO ORDER

Christian bookshops: All good Christian bookshops stock BRF publications. For your nearest stockist, please contact BRF.

POSTAGE AND PACKING CHARGES				
order value	UK	Europe	Surface	Air Mail
£7.00 & under	£1.25	£3.00	£3.50	£5.50
£7.01–£30.00	£2.25	£5.50	£6.50	£10.00
Over £30.00	free	prices on request		

Telephone: The BRF office is open between 09.15 and 17.30.
To place your order, phone 01865 319700; fax 01865 319701.

Web: Visit www.brf.org.uk

❑ Please do not send me further information about BRF publications.

BRF is a Registered Charity

ND0106